Economic Losses and Mitigation after an Employment Termination

Dwight Steward

Economic Losses and Mitigation after an Employment Termination

Theory, Applications, and Case Studies

palgrave
macmillan

Dwight Steward
EmployStats
Austin, TX, USA

ISBN 978-3-030-88363-8   ISBN 978-3-030-88364-5 (eBook)
https://doi.org/10.1007/978-3-030-88364-5

© The Editor(s) (if applicable) and The Author(s), under exclusive license to Springer Nature Switzerland AG 2022

This work is subject to copyright. All rights are solely and exclusively licensed by the Publisher, whether the whole or part of the material is concerned, specifically the rights of translation, reprinting, reuse of illustrations, recitation, broadcasting, reproduction on microfilms or in any other physical way, and transmission or information storage and retrieval, electronic adaptation, computer software, or by similar or dissimilar methodology now known or hereafter developed.

The use of general descriptive names, registered names, trademarks, service marks, etc. in this publication does not imply, even in the absence of a specific statement, that such names are exempt from the relevant protective laws and regulations and therefore free for general use.

The publisher, the authors and the editors are safe to assume that the advice and information in this book are believed to be true and accurate at the date of publication. Neither the publisher nor the authors or the editors give a warranty, expressed or implied, with respect to the material contained herein or for any errors or omissions that may have been made. The publisher remains neutral with regard to jurisdictional claims in published maps and institutional affiliations.

Cover illustration: © Harvey Loake

This Palgrave Macmillan imprint is published by the registered company Springer Nature Switzerland AG
The registered company address is: Gewerbestrasse 11, 6330 Cham, Switzerland

Acknowledgements

I would like to thank my incredible EmployStats support staff and research team for their assistance with the production of this book.

I would especially like to thank Carl McClain for his assistance with the literature review and research summaries. I would also like to thank Susie Wirtanen for her assistance with numerous calculations and case studies throughout the book. Finally, I would like to thank Matt Rigling for his assistance with the retirement section research.

Contents

Overview of Employment Economic Damage Models	1
But-for Employment Termination Projections	7
But-for Employment Termination Compensation	8
Employer Provided Fringe Benefits	12
Stock Based Compensation	13
Defined Benefit and Defined Contribution Retirement Plans	17
Employment Job Tenure Projections	21
Information Sources	24
Re-Employment and Job Search Activities	27
Job Search and Mitigation	28
Comparable Replacement Employment	29
Characteristics of a Diligent Job Search	31
Methods of Job Search	32
Analyzing the Plaintiff's Job Search Efforts	34
A Comparison of Job Search Efforts for Identical Plaintiffs	36
Measuring Individualized Employer Demand	43
Employer Demand Measurement Methodology	44
Plaintiff's Expected Unemployment Duration	47
Underemployment and Retirement	49
Interest Rate Discounting Front Pay Losses	51
Present Value and Interest Rate Discounting	52
Example Calculation	53

Insights from Labor Market Research and Data	57
Job Search and Mitigation Labor Market Research	57
Useful Labor Data Sources	68
Stock Based Employee Compensation	75
Case Study Background	77
Analysis of Plaintiff's Allegations	78
Conclusions	86
Employee Stock Options References	86
Analysis Information Requirements	89
Information Typically Needed	90
Guidelines on Collecting Information for Lost Earnings Analyses in Employment Termination Cases	90
Sample Employment Termination Case Information Checklist	91
Sample Plaintiff Interrogatory Questions	92
Case Study 1: Registered Nurse v. Health Science Center	95
In Brief	95
Background	96
Analysis	97
Case Study 2: Truck Driver v. Concrete Mixing Company	101
In Brief	101
Background	102
Analysis	102
Case Study 3: Fire Fighters' Association v. The City	107
In Brief	107
Background	108
Analysis	108
Case Study 4: Attorney v. Public Utility Employer	115
In Brief	116
Background	116
Analysis	117
Case Study 5: Medical Doctor v. Physician Group Partners	121
In Brief	121
Background	122
Analysis	123

Case Study 6: CFO v. Fintech Employer   127
In Brief   127
Background   128
Analysis   129

Case Study 7: VP of Business Development v. Energy Company   135
In Brief   135
Background   136
Analysis   138

Case Study 8: Duncan v. The City   141
In Brief   141
Background   142
Analysis   144

Index   151

About the Author

Dwight Steward, Ph.D. is a professional economist and the principal of EmployStats. EmployStats is a boutique economic consulting firm that provides economic research and expert witness services to legal, government, and business communities nationwide. EmployStats specializes in large data analysis projects involving employment class action lawsuits, injury and death litigation, consumer mass torts, and commercial lawsuits. Dwight has provided consultation, expert reports, and testimony in hundreds of cases nationwide. EmployStats has been successful in business since 1997 and has offices in Austin, TX, and Palo Alto, CA, and at www.employstats.com.

Dwight is a labor economist with over 20 years of extensive experience in teaching and researching the labor market analyses presented and discussed in this book. Dwight has taught dozens of courses in labor market economics and statistics to advanced undergraduate and graduate students at the University of Texas at Austin that cover the labor market issues such as unemployment and re-employment, expected job unemployment duration, job skill transferability in the labor market, and the determination of an employee's wage rate in the labor market.

In addition to university teaching of the labor market methodologies and labor market data, Dwight has also presented peer-reviewed labor economic research on these labor market methodologies and data at numerous major national economic conferences. Dwight has organized research panels on the labor market analysis of economic damages, employment, and re-employment in employment cases at numerous professional economic associations, including the American Economic Association (AEA) conferences.

In addition to his labor market teaching and writing, Dwight has provided trial testimony on labor market issues similar to those discussed in this book in Federal and State Courts across the country. His trial testimony experience includes Monica Hague v. University of Texas Health Science Center at San Antonio, in the United States District Court for the Western District of Texas, San Antonio Division, Civil Action No. SA-11-CA-1101-OG and in Michael Chatterton v. Beelman Ready Mix, Inc., in the Circuit of the Twentieth Judicial Circuit St. Clair County, Illinois, No. 14-L-221, and dozens of others. In addition, in Coleman et al. v. Newsom et al., United States District Court for the Eastern District of California, Dwight was appointed as a labor economist by the Court to assist the Court's Special Master. As a labor economist for The Court's Special Master, Dwight conducted a labor market availability and salary analysis to help the Court study the labor market issues in the Coleman v. Newsom case.

Dwight is an active community member and serves in a number of leadership positions. He is currently on the Board of Directors of The Boys and Girls Club of Austin and serves as the Midwest vice president of the National Association of Forensic Economics. Dwight is also a member of the Texas A&M University Statewide Police Racial Profiling Task Force and a former president of the University of Texas at Austin, Army ROTC Alumni Association.

Dwight is the author of three professional economics textbooks and was previously a Senior Lecturer in the Economics department at The University of Texas at Austin and was a visiting assistant professor in the Finance Department in the College of Business at Sam Houston State University in Huntsville, Texas. He served stateside in the U.S. Army as a field artillery officer during Operation Desert Storm and in the U.S. Army Reserves. Dwight obtained the rank of first Lt. and received an honorable discharge following the completion of his service.

Dwight holds a Ph.D. in Economics from the University of Iowa and a B.A. in Economics from the University of Texas at Austin. He completed his K-12 schooling in San Antonio, Texas. Dwight's hobbies include raising Hereford cattle and watching professional and collegiate sports.

LIST OF TABLES

Overview of Employment Economic Damage Models

Table 1	Economic damage model in employment termination case	5

But-for Employment Termination Projections

Table 1	Value of employer paid fringe benefits in March 2020 for selected employee groupings	13
Table 2	Value of a single employee stock option	16
Table 3	Number of years with current employer for selected years	23
Table 4	Number of Years with Current Employer, for 2018	23
Table 5	Number of years with current employer, by industry. Women 35–44, bachelor's degree	24

Interest Rate Discounting Front Pay Losses

Table 1	The present value of Plaintiff's front pay losses	54

Stock Based Employee Compensation

Table 1	Employee stock compensation at issue in breach of contract lawsuit	78
Table 2	Analysis of damages related to unawarded ESOs	81
Table 3	Defense expert's analysis of damage to outstanding vested ESOs using Hull-White model	82

Overview of Employment Economic Damage Models

Abstract The goal of this book is to provide a conceptual and practical discussion of the factors that comprise a standard economic damage model in an employment termination case. In this book, we discuss the economic factors and assumptions that comprise an economic damages model in an employment termination case. We also provide a discussion of the valuation of employee fringe benefits and employee stock option valuations. Background on the concept of discounting and discussions of the required information in employment cases are also provided.

Keywords Employment termination · Economic damage · But-for · Back pay · Front pay

Most Plaintiffs in employment termination cases will ultimately become re-employed. However, for some Plaintiffs the termination of their employment produces economic damage to their earnings, retirement pension, and fringe benefits. For other Plaintiffs, an employment termination causes little to no measurable economic harm. The individual Plaintiff's efforts and ability to regain comparable replacement employment is often the key difference between the two types of Plaintiffs.

© The Author(s), under exclusive license to Springer Nature Switzerland AG 2022
D. Steward, *Economic Losses and Mitigation after an Employment Termination*,
https://doi.org/10.1007/978-3-030-88364-5_1

Moreover, unlike in other types of cases, the Plaintiff's efforts to find re-employment, or what attorney's refer to as mitigation, is an important portion of the economic damage model in an employment termination case and needs to be directly considered in the analysis of any alleged back or front pay losses. In contrast to a case involving a person who is severely physically injured and unable to return to the work, the Plaintiff's efforts to obtain replacement employment following their employment termination directly affects the likelihood that the Plaintiff will become re-employed.

The goal of this book is to provide a conceptual and practical discussion of the factors that comprise a standard economic damage model in an employment termination case. In this book, we discuss the economic factors and assumptions that comprise an economic damages model in an employment termination case. We also provide a discussion of the valuation of employee fringe benefits and employee stock option valuations. Background on the concept of discounting and discussions of the required information in employment cases are also provided in this paper.

In wrongful employment termination cases, the Plaintiff typically alleges that the cessation of their employment with the Defendant has resulted in a loss of earnings and employer provided fringe benefits, such as health insurance and retirement. Conceptually, the goal of an economic analysis in a typical wrongful employment termination case is to compare the compensation that the Plaintiff would have received at the Defendant employer had their employment not been terminated to the compensation that the Plaintiff can now be reasonably expected to receive from replacement employment now that their employment with the Defendant employer has been terminated. The difference between these two compensation streams measures the Plaintiff's projected economic loss due to the alleged wrongful employment termination.

A typical economic damage analysis of the Plaintiff's lost earnings in an employment termination case involves several main parts. The parts of the analysis involve the Plaintiff's 'but-for' employment termination income, the Plaintiff's job search efforts and replacement employment, and discounting of future alleged losses, or front pay, to present value. The first part of the employment economic analysis involves determining the earnings, fringe benefits, and retirement income that the terminated employee would have received had he or she not been terminated by the defendant.

The projected earnings that the Plaintiff would have earned had their employment not been terminated by the Defendant is frequently referred to as the Plaintiff's 'but-for' employment termination earnings. The projection of earnings that the Plaintiff would have made at the Defendant but-for the alleged discrimination is made by examining company specific factors such as the Plaintiff's earnings history at the company, position at the company, education level and other factors related to the Plaintiffs position at the Defendant. Defendant company specific data on issues such as job advancement opportunities, expected job tenure and retirement are also typically utilized in determining the Plaintiff's but-for employment earnings potential at the Defendant employer.

The second portion of the economic damage calculation involves determining the compensation that the Plaintiff can now be expected to earn now that their employment at the Defendant employer has ended. This income is typically referred to as the Plaintiff's expected replacement employment income. In determining the Plaintiff's replacement employment income potential, factors such as the past earnings of the Plaintiff, types of job positions held prior to their employment with the Defendant, employer demand for the Plaintiff's skills and expertise, and post-employment termination job search efforts. The Plaintiff's job search efforts, as evidenced by their job search logs, emails and other related items are an important factor in determining their expected replacement income potential.

The third portion of the economic damage calculation involves determining the present value of any future alleged economic losses over the projected economic damage period. Factors such as the Plaintiff's expected job tenure with the employer/Defendant, job turnover trends, and employer demand for the Plaintiff's skill set are considered in the determination of the economic damage period. In the calculation, the present value of any alleged future losses takes into account what is referred to as the 'time value of money'. The underlying time value of money premise in the present value calculation is that a dollar received tomorrow is worth less than a dollar received today. This is because a dollar received today can be invested, or deposited in a bank account today that will earn interest and grow until the time the money is actually needed at a later date. Conversely, if the person receives a dollar tomorrow, or at a later date, they will not have the opportunity to earn interest on that money that they receive at the later date.

In the present value calculation, a higher present value interest rate discount factor results in a lower value for the Plaintiff's alleged future losses. For example, a present value interest rate discount factor of 5% will yield a lower value than a present value interest discount factor of 1%. When interest rates are higher, i.e. 5% in the example, the amount of interest that is foregone by not receiving the money today is greater than when interest rates are lower, i.e. 1% in the example. Conversely, and for the same reasons, a lower present value interest rate discount factor results in a higher value for the Plaintiff's future alleged losses.

In employment termination calculations, it is generally accepted practice to utilize a relatively low interest rate. All things being considered equal, higher interest rates, such as those that could be expected from investing in a company's stock, reflect underlying market factors including factors such as risk. Accordingly, a relatively low interest rate reflects a relatively low level of underlying risk. Courts have generally required that future damages be discounted to present value using a risk-free and below market rate interest rate and not interest rates associated with stocks or other equities. The present day value of the Plaintiff's alleged economic damages in employment cases is typically calculated using interest rate data from safe investments such as U.S. Treasury Bills, Bonds, and Notes.[1]

In employment termination cases, the economic damages are generally split into two parts called **back pay** and **front pay**. Back pay is generally defined as the losses that the Plaintiff incurs from the time that the employment termination occurred to the date of a report or other significant date, such as the date of trial. Back pay is typically calculated as the difference between the earnings that the Plaintiff could have been expected to earn at the employer/defendant and the actual and/or expected earnings from replacement employment. Interest is usually not included in the economist's calculation of back pay losses since pre-judgment interest is typically determined by the Court.

Front pay losses are the difference between the future wages that the Plaintiff would have been expected to have earned at employer/defendant

---

[1] Conceptually, the present value calculation involves determining how much money would have to be deposited in a relatively safe investment today to compensate the Plaintiff for the dollar income losses that the Plaintiff is expected to experience over the relevant economic damage period. The amount to be deposited in a safe investment, such as a U.S. treasury security, is called the present value of the future stream of income.

Table 1 Economic damage model in employment termination case

Damage time Period	But-for employment at defendant	Actual and expected replacement employment	Damage component
T_0: Date of termination T_1: Date of analysis (report or trial)	Part A: But-for expected past earnings from date of termination (T_0) to date of analysis (T_1)	Part B: Actual or expected past replacement earnings from date of termination (T_0) to date of analysis (T_1)	Back Pay = A - B
T_N: End of damages period	Part C: But-for expected future earnings from date of analysis (T_1) to end of damage period (T_N)	Part D: Expected replacement earnings from date of analysis (T_1) to end of damage period (T_N)	Front Pay = C - D
	Plaintiff's Alleged Economic Loss = Back Pay + Present Value(Front Pay)		

and their current expected future replacement earnings. Since the Plaintiff would not have earned the wages until some point in the future, these projected earnings are discounted by an appropriate interest rate discount factor and may take into account income taxes. Table 1 shows the different components of the economic damage model.

But-for Employment Termination Projections

Abstract The projected earnings that the Plaintiff would have earned had their employment not been terminated by the Defendant is frequently referred to as the Plaintiff's 'but-for' employment termination earnings. The projection of earnings that the Plaintiff would have made at the Defendant employer but-for the alleged discrimination is made by examining company specific factors such as the Plaintiff's earnings history at the company, position at the company, education level and other factors related to the Plaintiffs position at the Defendant. Defendant company specific data on issues such as job advancement opportunities, expected job tenure and retirement are also typically utilized in determining the Plaintiff's but-for employment earnings potential at the Defendant employer. This section discusses these issues.

Keywords Projected earnings · Fringe benefits · Stock based compensation · Retirement benefits · Tenure projections

The projected earnings that the Plaintiff would have earned had their employment not been terminated by the Defendant is frequently referred to as the Plaintiff's 'but-for' employment termination earnings. The projection of earnings that the Plaintiff would have made at the Defendant employer but-for the alleged discrimination is made by examining company specific factors such as the Plaintiff's earnings history at the company, position at the company, education level and other factors related to the Plaintiffs position at the Defendant. Defendant company specific data on issues such as job advancement opportunities, expected job tenure and retirement are also typically utilized in determining the Plaintiff's but-for employment earnings potential at the Defendant employer. This section discusses these issues.

In general, there are two principal questions that arise when studying the Plaintiff's employment prior to the termination of their employment with the Defendant. The first question is **what** would the Plaintiff have been reasonably expected to have earned in terms of monetary compensation and employer provided fringe benefits, such as health insurance and retirement, had they remained employed at the Defendant. The second question is **how long** could the Plaintiff have been reasonably expected to earn that level of compensation from the Defendant employer had their employment not been terminated?

Let's begin with the issue of a reasonable but-for employment termination compensation projection for the Plaintiff. Depending on the job, a typical Plaintiff can be expected to have a compensation package that is a mix of wages, such as salaries and commissions, and non-wage compensation, such as employer provided health benefits, employee stock options, Social Security employer payments, life insurance, and retirement contributions.

But-for Employment Termination Compensation

Generally, calculating a reasonable but-for employment termination compensation for the Plaintiff utilizes a historical earnings or similarly situated company specific approach, or a mix of the two approaches. The **historical earnings** approach uses the Plaintiff's historical wage information to project his or her but-for past earnings level. Use of the historical earnings methodology may be particularly appropriate in cases in which workers have a history of steady employment with the employer and a well-documented employment history. The historical earnings approach may involve using a relatively small swath of time such as the salary from the last few weeks or a longer time period such as the average of the last three to five years.

For instance, for some sales related occupations it may be appropriate to use the average of the last two to three years of earnings because the incomes of individuals in these types of jobs vary with their sales. Alternatively for an individual in a job position that receives consistent wage and salary increases, such as individuals on a set government or union pay scale, using the last year's salary combined with the historical growth rate experienced by the individual may by the most appropriate estimate.

The similarly-situated or **company specific** approach works in the same way, but instead of using an individual's actual earnings history, earnings levels are based on the average earnings for a group of workers that are similar to the person in question. The comparison group may be determined using labor market data and/or employer specific data. This approach may be particularly appropriate in cases in which the Plaintiff has been steadily employed within a single trade, industry or company.

Earnings levels and but-for growth rate projections based on the similarly-situated or company specific approach typically use occupational information from sources such as government surveys, empirical state labor force commission labor market data, employer pay grades, and job progression information. Generally speaking, because of differing labor demand, labor supply, and productivity factors, the average annual salary tends to vary across different occupational groups. However, similarly situated employees employed in similar labor markets tend to earn similar wages across different employers.

For some individuals, company specific information may be more useful for calculating the Plaintiff's but-for expected past earnings. For instance, for Plaintiffs whose salary is based heavily on sales and commissions, the pipeline of sales prospects and opportunities that the Plaintiff had in place at the time of the termination may be helpful for determining what they could have expected had they remained employed by the defendant. In cases, especially cases where the employment termination is part of a larger reduction in force and company reorganization, the earnings opportunities that the Plaintiff could have been expected to realize may be different from the opportunities that were in place when the Plaintiff was employed at the defendant. During reduction in force actions and re-organizations, management structures, sales territories and department alignments are frequently altered. In these instances, the company information provided by the defendant could be insightful.

Deposition testimony concerning the Plaintiff's work history can be insightful. A deposition excerpt from a bank business development officer is shown below. In the excerpts, the Plaintiff provides insights that are useful to the analysis of the Plaintiff's but-for employment termination project compensation

> Q: I did want to cover your employment before [Defendant] just briefly. Earlier, you said that you started working at [REDACTED EMPLOYER] in 1985 approximately.
> A: Correct.
> Q: And what did you do for [REDACTED EMPLOYER]?
> A: Variety of -- a variety of positions I held. I came in as a collector for loans. I then moved into underwriting for loans. I then moved into -- make sure I get this in sequential order as best I can. Assistant Manager of Sales. And then moved into Lobby Operations. Then I went to -- back to Loans Sales and Service. And then I went into Loan Administration.
> Q: Do you remember when you started as a loan collector for [REDACTED EMPLOYER], about what you were earning?
> A: $16,500 a year.
> Q: And what year did you leave?
> A: December, '01.
> Q: And about what were you making then?
> A: I estimate about 65; 65, 70 thousand.
> Q: And at [REDACTED EMPLOYER], did they have a pension?
> A: Yes.
> Q: So did you receive pension benefits through [REDACTED EMPLOYER]?
> A: I did.
> Q: So what did you do after [REDACTED EMPLOYER]?

Later in the deposition testimony the Plaintiff described a middle career job pivot from the banking industry. This testimony assists in determining the full range of jobs that are consistent with the Plaintiff's knowledge, experience, and expertise.

> A: I -- I went to the golfing industry, to become a certified golf instructor, and that was three years.
> Q: Is that something you had wanted to do? I mean, it's a change from financial services, correct?

A: It's a passion I had with regards to teaching, coaching, developing people, and I felt it was an opportunity to do it with the passion I had in the golf.
Q: And what was your compensation arrangement? Was it a salary, something else?
A: Commission. Commission per clinic or lesson.
Q: About how much did you make a year?
A: I would say probably eight grand total.
Q: Did you receive benefits? Medical benefits, retirement?
A: Actually I don't recall.
Q: Were you contributing to any sort of retirement account?
A: I don't believe so, no.

The Plaintiff later describes a pivot back to the banking industry. The middle career pivot, which reduced his level of experience in the banking industry, has a potential impact on the earnings that he could have expected to from the defendant but-for his employment termination.

Q: Why did you stop working in the golfing industry?
A: I wanted to get back into the banking industry.
Q: Where did you work next?
A: [REDACTED Credit Union].
Q: How long did you work there?
A: Seven months.
Q: What was your job title there?
A: Loan underwriter.
Q: What was your compensation?
A: 40 -- if I can remember correctly, $47,500.
Q: Did you receive medical benefits through the credit union?
A: Yes, ma'am.
Q: Did you contribute to a retirement account through the credit union?
A: Yes, I did.
Q: When you worked at [REDACTED Credit Union], were you paid a base salary?
A: Yes, ma'am.
Q: Was there any additional variable components, like a commission or a bonus?
A: No, ma'am.

Employer Provided Fringe Benefits

Fringe benefits are the non-wage benefits that an employer provides to its employees. Employer-provided benefits include life insurance, health insurance, retirement benefits, social security contributions, unemployment insurance, and worker's compensation insurance.

In addition to these fringe benefits, some employers may provide monetary allowances for items such as work-related clothing and automobile expenses that may directly benefit the individual employee. While there may be tax considerations or other offsetting expenses to consider, the value of these types of employer-provided job-related fringe benefits should be included if they are relevant.

Employer-provided fringe benefits generally are valued by estimating the monetary benefit to the individual employee who receives them. Conceptually, the monetary benefit to the individual employee is the amount the person would have to be paid to replace the employer-provided fringe benefits. The replacement value of the employer-provided benefits could be determined by calculating the amount it would cost the employee to obtain the benefits that they were provided by the employer before the injury or death occurred.

In practice, the valuation of the benefit that a person receives from employer-provided fringe benefits is performed by estimating the employer's direct cost of providing the benefits to the employee. The employer's direct cost estimate is used because it is difficult, or impossible in some instances, to determine the cost the employee would have to pay to replace the same fringe benefit package that the individual was receiving at the time of the injury or death. For instance, it is not usually possible for an individual person to buy unemployment insurance similar to the package offered by an employer.

A dollar value estimate can be obtained directly from the employer's records or government-collected labor market and employment data. More commonly, the economist uses government labor market and employment data to construct what is called a salary fringe benefit multiplier. A salary fringe benefit multiplier is a mathematical factor that shows the value of an employee's fringe benefits as a percentage of salary. The actual multiplier is based on the average cost of providing the benefits. Commonly used salary fringe benefit multipliers are derived from the U.S. Bureau of Labor Statistics (BLS) and other employer cost surveys.

Table 1 Value of employer paid fringe benefits in March 2020 for selected employee groupings

Income level	Management and business	Natural resources	Production and transportation	Sales
$50,000	$15,823	$16,449	$16,930	$11,862
$75,000	$23,734	$24,674	$25,395	$17,793
$100,000	$31,645	$32,899	$33,860	$23,724
$150,000	$47,468	$49,348	$50,790	$35,585
$200,000	$63,290	$65,797	$67,720	$47,447

Source U.S. Bureau of Labor Statistics, Employer Costs for Employee Compensation

For example, according to BLS studies and data, for a person working in a sales sector job, the value of employer-provided health insurance, life insurance, and other non-wage fringe benefits is equal to approximately 23.7% of the person's salary. Table 1 provides an example of the dollar value of the employer-provided benefits for employees in various sectors. Note that the dollar values for some fringe benefits, such as retirement benefits, may vary by income level, while other employer-provided benefits, such as health insurance, do not.

STOCK BASED COMPENSATION

Stock based compensation is another component of pay for some individuals. In some cases, the terminated Plaintiff may have been in a job position that awarded employee stock options (ESOs) or stock grants. Other employees may have been enrolled in plans that made them eligible for participation in the employer's stock purchase plans. In this section, the basics of ESO's are discussed. A more detailed discussion of employee stock option plans and other types of stock based compensation is provided in a later section of this book.

The deposition testimony excerpt below is that of a Human Resources Representative for a large energy company in an employment discrimination lawsuit involving a former employee. The employee was an executive and received stock based compensation as part of their overal compensation package.

Q: Does [REDACTED EMPLOYER] have a plan for employees to buy stocks?
A: Yes.
Q: Okay. What is that plan?
A: It's an employee stock purchase plan where you can allocate a certain percentage of your salary, and then your stocks that you retain for two years are matched in January.
Q: And you do that every year?
A: Yes.
Q: Someone can do that every year?
A: You can enroll or change your enrollment, yes. But you have to keep the stocks for two years before they can be matched.
Q: Does the company have an internal running list of employees who want retirement packages?
A: No.
Q: Do you know kind of offhand who those employees are?
A: No, we don't offer retirement packages.

As in the sample case above, stock based incentives are fairly common forms of compensation. Specifically when a person is granted ESOs by an employer, that employee receives the right to purchase a set number of shares of the employer's stock at a predetermined price. The predetermined price is called the **grant price**. The employee generally must meet certain conditions before he or she can exercise the stock options, i.e. purchase the stock.

The employee usually must be with the employer for a certain amount of time, called a vesting period. Additionally, the employee's stock option rights expire within a set time period, usually within 10 years. The employee's stock purchase rights also generally expire after the person leaves the employment of the issuing company.

Subject to these restrictions, the employee may choose to purchase the employer's stock at his or her discretion. The employee makes money if he or she is able to exercise the stock option at the agreed upon grant price, and then sell the employer's stock at a higher market price. The employee does not have to exercise the option. As a result, employees are not at risk of losing money if the stock price does not exceed the agreed-upon purchase price.

Regardless of the type of ESOs, the issue in an employment termination case is to determine the value to the employee of having the right to purchase the company's stock. That is, how much would a person pay for the right to purchase the ESO grant? Keep in mind when valuing the ESO that the goal is not the value of the underlying stock, but instead, it is the value of the employee stock option. Clearly, the two are related, but are not the same.

The value of an employee's stock is a function of a number of factors. These factors include the employer's stock price, the grant price, and the exercise restrictions that the employer has placed upon the ESO grants. The value of an employee's stock option grant is affected by economic variables such as the interest rate in the economy, the employee turnover rate of the company, and the anticipated variability of the stock price. The value of the ESO will almost always be less than the market value of the stock option because of the exercise restrictions placed on the employee's ownership of the option.

In essence, the valuation of an ESO implicitly considers all the possible stock price outcomes that could occur and places a value on the ESO based on these possible stock price outcomes. The valuation is done using well-known mathematical models. Usually, the valuation of the stock options that the terminated employee would have received is derived using standard mathematical models such as the Black-Scholes or Binomial Tree model. These mathematical models return the value of each ESO that the person held at the time of their termination or that would have been awarded in the future. For some companies, the ESO value from these mathematical model valuations can be found in the company's filings with the Securities Exchange Commission.

Table 2 shows the values of a hypothetical employee's stock option. This table presents the dollar value a person would pay for the right to purchase a share of the employer's stock, at the predetermined grant price, at some date in the next eight years. As the table shows, the value of a single ESO changes as the grant price and the underlying price of the employer's stock change. Again, remember the value of the ESO is not the value of the employer's underlying stock, but, instead, it is the value of the employee's stock option grant. Also remember that the valuations are not simply the investment return derived from the difference between the grant price and the price of the employer stock price as of the day of the valuation. Instead, the valuation takes into account the range of likely investment returns given the stock price's volatility.

For instance, consider a hypothetical firm whose stock presently trades at $10 per share. Further, the stock option grant price is $5 and may be

Table 2 Value of a single employee stock option

		Price of Employer Stock			
		$1	$5	$10	$20
ESO Grant Price	$1	$0.45	$4.26	$9.25	$19.24
	$5	$0.05	$2.23	$6.61	$16.32
	$10	$0.01	$1.15	$4.46	$13.23
	$20	$0.00	$0.41	$2.30	$8.93
	$30	$0.00	$0.19	$1.33	$6.29
	$40	$0.00	$0.10	$0.83	$4.59
	$50	$0.00	$0.06	$0.55	$3.45

Notes The ESO grant price is the price at which the employee can purchase the employer's stock. The price of the employer's stock is the price at which the stock is trading in the stock market as of the day the ESO is valued. It is assumed that the option has vested at the time the ESO is valued and there are 8 years until expiration. The table does not include adjustments for such things as lack of company marketability
Source Value Line database; http://pages.stern.nyu.edu/~adamodar/

exercised at any time within the next eight years. The value of such an ESO is $6.61 in this example.

This valuation takes into account the fact that if the person purchases the ESO, the employer's stock may or may not exceed the grant price over the next eight years that remain on the ESO. Intuitively, the lower the grant price, or predetermined purchase price set by the employer, the higher the price the hypothetical person would pay for the ESO.

In addition to ESOs, it is also possible that the terminated employee was eligible for or participated in an employee stock purchase plan. Employee stock purchase plans allow the employee to purchase the employer's stock at a discounted rate. Employee stock purchase plans are valued in a similar fashion as ESOs since there is no guarantee that the stock price will remain at this level. Most employee stock purchase plans impose restrictions on reselling the stock purchased under the plan.

The discount on the stock price varies by employer, but it tends to be in the area of around 15–20% of the market price. With employee stock purchase plans, the employee makes money if he or she is able to sell the discounted stock in the future at a price higher than the purchase price. In most employee stock purchase plans, there are usually certain restrictions on how soon and/or how much the employee can sell the purchased stocks. There are valuation models for stock purchase plans.

However, since participation in the plan requires a purchase on the part of the employee, the potential value associated with participation tends to be lower than that associated with employee stock option plans.

Guidelines on employee stock options and employee stock purchase plans

1. Valuations based on the best case scenario of the employer's stock price are not very informative. Although the employee will not lose money, he or she may not necessarily make money as the employer stock price may not exceed the grant price during the allotted time in the option.
2. An employee stock option that is currently "underwater," i.e. the grant price is higher than the market price, is not necessarily valueless. The option may still be valuable if there is sufficient probability that the stock price will increase in the future.
3. All other factors remaining equal, the higher the volatility, i.e. the more the employer's stock price fluctuates, the higher the value of the employee stock option. This is because a naturally larger range of stock price values makes larger gains more likely.
4. Most employee stock option plans will only vest a certain percentage of options per year.
5. Most employee stock option plans will have a provision that terminates the option automatically within a set period, commonly 90 days, of a not-for-cause employment termination.
6. Although grant prices are typically set at the end of a fiscal or calendar year, some employers have been known to use special rules for setting grant prices, such as backdating to the lowest price over a given window of time.

In addition to ESO's, other stock based compensation includes, employee stock grant units, and employee stock purchase programs. These are discussed in a later section of the book.

Defined Benefit and Defined Contribution Retirement Plans

Retirement benefits are an important part of the compensation package for a number of Plaintiffs. The value of retirement benefits generally depends on a reliable projection of the Plaintiff's expected retirement age. In some instances, an average retirement age is appropriate, in other cases the individual's eligibility age for Social Security retirement is appropriate. In still other cases, neither is appropriate and instead an employer specific retirement is most relevant to the analysis of the Plaintiff's retirement benefits.

Deposition testimony from company representatives can be particularly insightful and can provide information concerning the Plaintiff's likely retirement age had the Plaintiff stayed employed by the Defendant. The deposition transcript excerpt below provides examples of such testimony.

Deposition of Director of US and Mexico Human Resources for a large energy company

Q: What about 57 mean retirement eligibility?
A: That's actually a system calculation, and it's based on an average. So, our team in -- that provides data from SAP, this is actually just based on average retirement ages across the organization.

Additional testimony from company employees that have extensive and personal experience with the Plaintiff's job position with the Defendant may also help to determine the responsibilities and scope of job the Plaintiff held. Such testimony may come from Hiring and Recruiting managers with in-depth knowledge of the position and requirements of the position. Testimony from an individual that has held the Plaintiff's job position is also insightful. This information can come in different forms including deposition testimony, telephone interviews, or declarations.

Some employers provide their employees with **defined benefit** programs, commonly referred to as employee pension plans. Typically, in a defined benefit pension plan, the employer will promise to pay a specified benefit payment amount, or potentially a lump sum, to the employee upon the employee's retirement. The amount of the pension benefit paid by the employer is based on a number of factors including the employee's historical earnings at the company, years of service or tenure at the employer, and potentially other employer-specific factors. The exact components of the defined benefit pension plan are described in detail in most employer pension plan handbooks or human resource manuals.

The employer's handbook will detail the formula that the company uses to calculate the employee's defined benefit payment, as well as the rules of eligibility for the program. In general, the defined benefit formula will multiply an average of the employee's highest historical earnings by a set percentage and the employee's tenure or years of service at the company. In most cases, the employee must work for the company and be a member of the pension program for a set number of years before they are eligible to receive the defined benefit compensation at retirement.

The example below shows a typical retirement pension calculation. Typical retirement pension formula:

Average Salary = Average of Three Highest Annual Salaries
Total Percent = Total Years of Service Credit × 2.3%
Annual Annuity = Total Percent x Average Salary
Monthly Annuity = Annual Annuity÷12

Consider an employee who worked for 15 years, and their highest salaries were $78,000, $80,000, and $82,000. Using the formulas listed above, the employee's pension would be calculated as:

Average Salary = ($78,000 + $80,000 + $82,000)/3 = $80,000
Total Percent = 15 × 0.023 = 0.345 = 34.5%
Annual Annuity = 0.345 x $80,000 = $27,600
Monthly Annuity = $27,600/12 = $2,300

As shown, this employee would be expected to receive a monthly defined benefit of $2,300, from the disbursement date through the remainder of their life. Many defined benefit retirement plans allow the employee to select to have their benefits transfer to another individual in the event of their death.

In these company's defined benefit plans, the employee is offered a survivor's option where the employee can elect to receive a reduced annuity for life, that is then paid to a surviving beneficiary upon the employee's death. In many plans, in order for a surviving beneficiary to receive an employee's defined benefit payment, the employee must have elected into the survivor defined benefit program prior to their retirement. It should also be noted that the payments under a survivors defined benefit plan will be less than the typical defined benefit plan with no survivors benefits.

In contrast to a defined benefit retirement plan, in a **defined contribution** retirement plan, the employee will contribute a fixed amount or percentage of their paychecks to an account intended to fund their retirement. The employee's company will, at times, match a portion of the employee contributions as an added benefit. Participation in a defined contribution retirement plan is both voluntary and self-directed, as opposed to a defined benefit retirement plan in which retirement income is guaranteed by an employer. Defined contribution retirement plans have become more prevalent in the workforce because they are less expensive to employers than other types of retirement plans. These plans are also popular with employees because they allow participants to contribute to their retirement with pre-tax dollars and reduce their income tax bill and allow the employee to choose their contributions with flexibility.

There are several different types of defined contribution retirement plans that employer's may sponsor for their employees. The most common type of defined contribution plan is a 401(k), where participants defer a portion of their pre-tax salary to the plan and the company may match the contribution as an added benefit. A 401(k) does have yearly contribution limits and in 2019, for example, the most a participant can contribute to their 401(k) plan was $19,000 or $25,000 for individuals age 50 and over. A 403(b) retirement plan is very similar to a 401(k) retirement plan. The key difference is the type of employer offering the plan. While a 401(k) plan is offered by for-profit companies, a 403(b) plan is offered to employees of non-profit organizations. An additional employer sponsored defined contribution retirement plan is a Savings Incentive Match Plan for Employees ('SIMPLE') IRA. A SIMPLE IRA is generally offered by smaller employers and allows a participant to make tax-deductible contributions and allows the employer to make matching contributions up to 3% of the employee's salary or nonelective contributions. For 2019, the annual contribution limit for SIMPLE IRA's was $13,000. Defined contribution retirement plans are controlled completely by the participant to manage through investment or withdrawals.

Suppose a company offers a 401(k) retirement plan to their employees. The formula for calculating the participants benefit would be simply the following:

Total contribution of 401(k) = Gross Pay (x) Percent Employee Contribution (+) Gross Pay (x) Percent Employer Contribution

For these examples, the employer matches the employees contributions up to 5% of their salary at the time. If the employee was earning $2,000 per bi-weekly pay period, their defined contribution each paycheck would be the following based on the employee's elected contributions:

Total contribution of 401(k) = ($2,000 x 0.05) + ($2,000 x 0.05)
= $200 per pay period

Total contribution of 401(k) = ($2,000 x 0.08) + ($2,000 x 0.05) = $260 per pay period

In the second example, the employee has elected to contribute an additional 3 percent of their pre-tax earnings to their retirement account, however the max employee contribution will not exceed 5% under this example. These types of contributions would continue so long as the employee remained employed and continued participating in the retirement plan.

Employment Job Tenure Projections

In addition to determining what compensation the Plaintiff could have been reasonably expected to earn, employment damage analyses require a projection as to how long the Plaintiff could have been reasonably expected to earn that level of compensation from the Defendant. In general, a number of factors make it unreasonable to assume that a Plaintiff's employment damages will continue to go over the entire span of a person's working life expectancy. Labor market factors such as job turnover, company reorganizations, and natural attrition make it unreasonable to assume that an individual Plaintiff would have remained employed at the Defendant employer for the remainder of their expected working life.

Accordingly, general work life expectancy tables for the labor market, such as those based on U.S. Bureau of Labor Statistics data, are not typically utilized in employment cases. Instead, company specific information and/or occupation specific labor and employment data is often more informative in employment termination cases. For instance, work life estimates based on U.S. Bureau of Labor data suggest that a female individual with a college education who is age 35 would be expected to work an additional 24.3 years. Unlike a loss of earnings capacity analysis in an injury or wrongful death case, it is unreasonable to assume that the 35 year old Plaintiff would have remained employed at the Defendant employer for the next 30 years had their employment not been allegedly wrongfully terminated. For instance, labor market data from the BLS shows that the typical average job tenure at one specific employer for persons aged 30–35, is approximately five years, which is clearly not consistent with economic damages that continue over the person's entire expected working life.

Similarly, there are numerous factors that make it unlikely that more experienced workers and those with more time at a single employer, will incur a working life level of economic damages. For instance, in companies that provide defined benefit retirements, some employees find that it is financially beneficial for them to retire and take their pension well in advance of the working life expectancy that would be suggested by U.S. BLS data.

In other jobs the expected or average time in the job position is dictated by the occupation, position at the company or the nature of the work. For instance, some jobs because of the level of physical and mental stress tend to have shorter time in job tenures at a given employer than other job positions that may be less stressful and taxing. Other jobs may have their average employment tenure limited by an employment contract or other agreement. In any event, general worklife tables, which are more typical in injury and wrongful death type economic loss calculations, are not as informative as company or occupation specific employment data sources.

Well, in the event the Plaintiff is projected to incur future economic losses, how long should the losses go on into the future? As described above, in some employment cases, it can be difficult to make economic assumptions that an individual Plaintiff's losses will go on forever or even throughout the person's entire working life. Alternatively, for some employees it may be reasonable to assume that the Plaintiff's economic losses will continue over some period of the Plaintiff's expected work life. The BLS collects information on employee job tenure through the Current Population Survey (CPS), by asking employees how long they have been employed with their current employer (in years).

If a Plaintiff asserts they would have continued with their present employer, but-for their termination, job tenure is a vital piece of information for estimating a Plaintiff's economic losses. The average employee, after a certain number of years, changes employers or exits the labor force. If an employee has already worked for an employer for several years beyond the average job tenure for their given occupation, then it is reasonable to expect their economic losses would not extend indefinitely. Job tenure varies by several different factors, for example by type of job position. Table 3 shows the average duration of employment in recent years among private and public sector employers.

For instance, government employees report longer tenure with their employers than private sector workers. In Table 3, the average private

Table 3 Number of years with current employer for selected years

Type	January 2014	January 2016	January 2018
All employees	7.96	7.77	7.81
Private sector	7.57	7.39	7.50
Public sector	10.24	10.01	9.70

Source U.S. Bureau of Labor Statistics

sector employee surveyed in 2018 had been working with their present employer for 7.5 years, while the average public sector employee had been working with their present employer for 9.7 years. For an employment termination case, a more detailed analysis would more closely represent the Plaintiff's actual experience. In this instance, to derive that median job tenure, calculations would consider relevant demographic and employment factors. For example, on average, older employees tend to have longer average job tenure than younger employees; on average, male employees tend to have longer average job tenure than female employees. Other important factors would include prior education, occupation, and industry.

For example, Table 4 shows the average duration of employment among men at different years of age at different levels of education.

In employment termination cases, information on job tenure should closely match the demographic characteristics of the Plaintiff. The more factors a job tenure analysis controls for, the more accurate an estimate would be for the job tenure of an employee comparable to the Plaintiff in

Table 4 Number of Years with Current Employer, for 2018

Education level	25–34 years	35–44 years	45–54 years	55–64 years
Less than a high school diploma	3.59	5.80	8.59	11.57
High school graduates, no college	3.76	6.80	10.66	13.83
Some college, no degree	3.37	6.65	10.26	12.98
Associates degree	3.95	6.79	10.54	13.18
Bachelor's degree only	3.48	7.07	10.44	13.15
Advanced degree	3.27	6.53	10.03	14.24

Source U.S. Bureau of Labor Statistics

Table 5 Number of years with current employer, by industry. Women 35–44, bachelor's degree

Example industries	January 2018
Elementary and secondary schools	7.03
Hospitals	7.55
Computer and data processing services	5.69
Real estate, including real estate-insurance	6.12
Eating and drinking places	4.72
Justice, public order, and safety	9.40
Accounting, auditing, and bookkeeping services	6.60
Research, development, and testing services	8.16

Source U.S. Bureau of Labor Statistics

a given industry. One example: what is the average job tenure of women between the ages of 35 and 44, with a bachelor's degree, in different industries? Table 5 shows some examples.

From Table 3, the data confirm general trends that one hears in anecdotal evidence. For example, employees in public sector industries (such as policing) tend to have longer job tenures than workers in private sector industries. Anecdotally, employees within tech industries (such as computer and data processing services), tend to have higher turnover than established professional industries like Accounting. Based on the data above in Table 5, women within tech or computer industries tend to have shorter job tenures than women working in other industries. The notable exception is the restaurant and food service industry, known for shorter job tenures.

INFORMATION SOURCES

Projections concerning the Plaintiff's employment with the Defendant are based on a number of information sources. These include information provided by the employer such as payroll records, retirement plan documents, pay statements, job descriptions, and Plaintiff personnel records. Other information such as personal tax returns and pay statements may be provided by the Plaintiff themself. Court records including interrogatories, production documents, and deposition testimony of the Plaintiff and key defendant employer personnel is also often utilized in the employment economic damage calculations.

The exact Information requirements for any given economic analysis will depend on the facts and circumstances of the case. Some general guidelines are found below.

- When possible, documents should be collected directly from the government agency and employer. Not all employees maintain a full set of pay stubs or financial records for the required number of years.
- Use multiple data sources to corroborate the financial picture. For example, use the 1040 tax return statement in conjunction with the W-2 wage and income statements. Looking at multiple sets of information allows for the separation of the income of multiple filers. Comparing the entries on both sets of documents will also enable the isolation and removal of income that is inappropriately reducing or increasing the subject's projected earnings.
- Valuation of retirement accounts will generally require a detailed employee benefits handbook. Obtain the summary plan description for the retirement plan.
- If possible, the cost of providing benefits should be directly obtained from the employer. The actual benefits data can provide an alternative to the standard salary multiplier measure, which is based on the average employer cost of providing benefits.
- It is important to obtain information from the years that best describe the subject's earnings potential during the time at issue to obtain an accurate projection of the earnings that the Plaintiff could have reasonably expected to earn from the Defendant. For some cases, this may be three years of historical data, but in other instances it may be a shorter time period.

More detailed discussion of data and information requirements in economic analyses of employment damages is provided in a later chapter.

Re-Employment and Job Search Activities

Abstract The Plaintiff's ability to regain comparable employment following an employment termination is often the principal issue in an employment case. In general, the Plaintiff's re-employment ability will depend on the effort that the individual puts into the job search efforts and employer demand for the individual Plaintiff's skill set. This chapter provides a high level conceptual overview of the factors that go into a re-employment projection. The following chapters present a more detailed discussion of job search and individualized employer demand evaluations.

Keywords Re-employment · Mitigation analysis · Comparable replacement · Diligent job search · Labor market

The Plaintiff's ability to regain comparable employment following an employment termination is often the principal issue in an employment case. In general, the Plaintiff's re-employment ability will depend on the effort that the individual puts into the job search efforts and employer demand for the individual Plaintiff's skill set. This chapter provides a high level conceptual overview of the factors that go into a re-employment projection. The following chapters present a more detailed discussion of job search and individualized employer demand evaluations.

© The Author(s), under exclusive license to Springer Nature Switzerland AG 2022
D. Steward, *Economic Losses and Mitigation after an Employment Termination*,
https://doi.org/10.1007/978-3-030-88364-5_3

Job Search and Mitigation

In an employment termination case, the Plaintiff generally has the duty to mitigate their economic losses by attempting to obtain comparable employment following their employment termination. Accordingly, unlike other types of lawsuits, such as personal injury cases involving individuals, an evaluation of the Plaintiff's job search efforts is an important part of an analysis of the Plaintiff's alleged economic damages in an employment case. In principle, an evaluation of the Plaintiff's post-termination job search evidence, such as job applications, job search logs and Plaintiff testimony, can provide insights into the diligence of the Plaintiff's required job search and consequently the Plaintiff's duty to mitigate their economic damages.

In practice, an evaluation of the Plaintiff's post-employment termination job search can be involved and require significant analysis. In many instances, the mitigation analysis is fundamentally impacted by the definition of a comparable job for the Plaintiff. The concept of a comparable replacement job has specific legal and economic meanings in an employment case. Employment case law generally establishes a comparable replacement job as one that is 'substantively similar to one that the Plaintiff held prior to their employment termination'. In some cases where the Plaintiff has alleged lost back and front pay, Plaintiffs will argue that even though their replacement job does not pay as much as they earned with the Defendant, they have met their duty to mitigate their damages by finding a job that is substantively similar because the duties and required skill set is substantively similar to the one that they held with the Defendant. In other instances, Defendants will attempt to show that the Plaintiff is underemployed and has not sufficiently mitigated their damages by illustrating that the Plaintiff's replacement job is in a new occupation, at a lower professional level or otherwise not substantively similar to the one that the Plaintiff held while employed with the Defendant.

In general, Courts have found that while a comparable job does not have to have the same job title as the one Plaintiff held while employed with the defendant, the job needs to utilize the same overall skill set that the Plaintiff held while employed with the Defendant. While comparability does not appear to require that the Plaintiff make the amount of money as they earned while employed with the Defendant, Courts have also stated that the compensation received by the Plaintiffs needs to be in line with that level of compensation. In practice, the determination of comparability of the Plaintiff's replacement job is often a heated point of contention in employment litigation.

COMPARABLE REPLACEMENT EMPLOYMENT

From a labor market perspective, a comparable job can be evaluated by examining three main areas of the job: duties and responsibilities, salary and compensation, and geographical location. The first area involves examining the day-to-day and overall duties and responsibilities of the Plaintiffs replacement job and the one that they held while employed with the Defendant. While the replacement and lost job position do not have to have the same job title, the duties and responsibilities of the replacement job should be similar, related, or transferable from the previous position held at the Defendant employer.

For instance, consider a Plaintiff who previously worked as a Mortgage Loan Originator at the Defendant's mortgage company. As a Mortgage Loan Originator, the Plaintiff's duties and responsibilities involved obtaining documents and information from borrowers and the home seller that would be used by underwriting and at other stages of the loan process. Following their employment termination at the Defendant's mortgage company, the Plaintiff obtained replacement employment at another mortgage company as a Mortgage Loan Processor. As a Mortgage Loan Processor, the Plaintiff's duties and responsibilities involved interacting with Loan Originators, lenders, and other individuals to produce the actual mortgage product for the customer and borrower.

In this example, the duties, responsibilities, and required skill set of the Plaintiff's replacement job and the job held at the Defendant are similar, related and transferable. The skill set and knowledge of the mortgage process is similar and related; in essence the two job positions are simply at different parts of the mortgage production chain. Moreover, many of the skills, while different, are transferable to the Plaintiff's replacement employment.

The conceptual framework for analyzing the concept of if a job is comparable is shown below.

1. Are duties, responsibilities of the job lost due to employment termination are the same, similar, related or transferable as the replacement job?

    a. Replacement job does not have to have the same job tile
    b. A related job can be in the same general job field (i.e. loan originator, loan processor)
    c. A comparable job can be one that utilizes the transferable skills used in the job at issue at the defendant-employer. (For example, a licensed attorney could transfer those to non-law based positions that require knowledge of the law and legal concepts).
2. Is the salary and compensation of the replacement job substantially similar to the job lost as a result of the employment termination?
    a. Important to consider the entire package including salary, benefits, and any other form of compensation received by the employee, such as stock options
    b. Some individuals will take lower earnings for less variation in earnings. Other individuals will take higher non-cash benefits, such as a defined benefit pension, over monetary pay.
    c. Working conditions may also be an issue. Some people take lower pay to be in a geographic area or professional area that they view as desirable.
3. Is the replacement job geographically comparable to the one that was lost due to the employment termination?
    a. The job does not have to be in the same city
        i. Can be in close proximity or reasonable range
        ii. Can be in areas that the Plaintiff was looking for work. Job search records of the Plaintiffs is a good starting point for determining the geographical boundaries of the Plaintiffs job search and labor market
    b. Shift to remote work has impacted the labor market. Many job positions that were not traditionally remote have become so.

Additionally, post-employment termination job search limitations that the Plaintiff is alleged to have faced may also need to be considered. For instance, in some cases the Plaintiff may allege that a vocational, physical, or psychological impairment related to the employment termination event may limit the types of employment that they feel that they are capable of holding and performing. In other cases, Plaintiffs allege and/or present evidence that certain events surrounding the employment termination have resulted in psychological limitations, such as PTSD, that prevents them from successfully obtaining and performing the job that they previously held with the Defendant. In these instances, the evaluation of other medical or vocational experts may be needed in order to obtain a clearer picture of the Plaintiff's post-employment job search activities.

CHARACTERISTICS OF A DILIGENT JOB SEARCH

The job search of a Plaintiff who is diligently attempting to obtain post-employment termination employment will generally exhibit a number of overarching characteristics. These characteristics are discussed below. Examples of analyzing a Plaintiff's job search are provided later in this chapter and in the case examples later in this book.

A first, and somewhat obvious characteristic of a diligent job search, is that the Plaintiff will put an appropriate amount of time into their job search for replacement employment. The appropriate amount of job search time will depend on a number of factors such as the Plaintiff's education level and type of replacement job that they are seeking. A diligent job search will be consistent over time and will commence relatively soon, if not before, the Plaintiff's employment ends with the defendant employer.

Second a diligent job search is that the Plaintiff's job search will be occupationally broad and sufficiently geographically expansive. That is, the Plaintiff will tend to look for not only the same job that they held at the time of their employment termination, but will also seek employment in jobs that are related, and demand a similar skill set, as the one they previously held. The qualifications and skill sets that a job seeker has is not typically limited to only one job and the person could apply to many different job positions in different industries.

Third, a job seeker that is diligently seeking employment would be expected to use all of the job search resources they have available to find a job. There are a number of ways that Plaintiffs go about finding replacement employment following an employment termination. These methods include searching electronic job posting boards, attending job fairs, and searching job postings in trade industry and general publications. Networking with colleagues and friends is also a common method by which individuals obtain replacement employment following a job termination.

The Plaintiff's job search evidence and mitigation attempts is often a major point of contention in an employment termination case. Some argue that the testimony of the Plaintiff alone may be used as sufficient evidence of an adequate job search and of the Plaintiff's attempt to mitigate their damages. That is, it is argued, that testimony by the Plaintiff that documents elements such as the number of jobs and types of jobs applied for following their termination may be sufficient to show the effort that the Plaintiff put forward in finding a new job position.

Some also argue that Plaintiff testimony may be useful for highlighting and bringing forth the issues that the Plaintiff may have had finding subsequent employment that are the result of the allegations in the case. For instance, some cases argue that the Defendant effectively limited the Plaintiff's job opportunities by talking bad or defaming the individual to other potential employers either directly or through negative information put out through various sources.

Labor market data is extremely useful in analyzing these types of allegations and the Plaintiff's job search efforts. Labor market data shows how individuals that are sufficiently similar to the Plaintiff have searched for replacement jobs following a job loss. While employment termination cases are unique in a lot of ways, they are also the same in a lot of ways from an analytical standpoint. Examining how other individuals find jobs and search for replacement jobs provides the Court and the trier of fact useful information and context by which to understand the particular Plaintiff's job search efforts.

In some cases a Plaintiff's job search analysis factors will be complicated by factors related to a Plaintiff's post-termination medical condition. It is possible that in some instances, the Plaintiff's ability to perform certain job positions, possibly including the one that the Plaintiff held at the time of their employment was terminated by the Defendant may be limited by a medical condition of some sort. In these instances, the Plaintiff job search analysis will likely need to account for the Plaintiff's medical situation in some appropriate manner. Testimony by a medical doctor or vocational rehabilitation expert may be necessary in some of these instances.

Methods of Job Search

There are a number of ways that Plaintiffs go about finding replacement employment following an employment termination. These methods include searching electronic job posting boards, attending job fairs, and searching job postings in trade industry and general publications. Networking with colleagues and friends is also a common method by which individuals obtain replacement employment following a job termination.

A study of job search methods performed by a major job posting internet site revealed a number of insights regarding how individuals search for jobs. In the study, which was a survey of individuals that were looking for work, the job seekers shared their preferred methods of searching for job opportunities. The study found the majority of job seekers preferred finding job opportunities through online methods such as internet job posting boards and employer websites. The survey also found that approximately 54% of individuals preferred working with recruiters and staffing agencies. Additionally approximately 20% of individuals responded that they utilized social media to obtain information about job opportunities.

The methods by which individuals search for jobs also tends to relate to the type of job they are looking to obtain. Individuals who are searching for jobs that require less specialized skills, experience, or expertise will tend to rely on a wider range of search methods. Recent high school and college graduates and individuals with skills that are more transferable across different occupations for instance, will tend to use methods such as electronic job posting boards, social media, networking, and attend in person job fairs to pursue job opportunities in various different industries. In part this is due to the fact that employers who are seeking more broadly skilled individuals will tend to broadcast their job opportunities more widely and across various avenues in order to fill their job openings. Employers who are looking to fill these types of positions tend to be more interested in finding the right fit for the position and company culture and will generally have an employee on-boarding process that will allow the employer to match and adapt the individual's skill set to the employer's needs.

Alternatively, individuals who are searching for job positions that require more specialized skills, experience, and expertise will tend to rely on different job search methods than those with less specialized employment backgrounds. For instance, individuals in some professions such as those that require a significant amount of formal education and specialized expertise, will tend to rely more on industry job placement resources and professional networking than professions that do not require as much formal education. Regardless of education level, individuals with job expertise that is more transferable across different types of industries and employers will tend to have a higher utilization of national electronic job search boards and employer driven job placement programs such as company websites and multi-employer recruitment job fairs.

Individuals in occupations that are extremely specialized and those that are searching for top level job positions with an employer will tend to have a higher utilization of employee placement firms, recruiters, and executive search firms. These types of employee placement firms may focus on the placement of certain professionals, such civil engineers or accountants. Other employment placement firms may be focused on the placement of individuals, regardless of their occupation, who work in a specific industry. Since the employment placement firm earns its profits by successfully placing individuals, the use of employee placement firms can be advantageous to the job seeking employee and the company seeking a candidate in the appropriate settings.

Analyzing the Plaintiff's Job Search Efforts

So in practice, what does a typical diligent job search look like? As was discussed earlier in this chapter, there are several characteristics that make up a diligent post-employment termination job search. First, a Plaintiff that is diligently looking for replacement employment will put in effort.

Of course the definition of effort depends on the Plaintiff's particular labor market and factors such as employer demand for the Plaintiff's knowledge, skills and abilities. It is reasonable to expect that a diligent job seeking Plaintiff will at a minimum apply to at least as many job positions as would be required to obtain state or local unemployment insurance benefits. Some states and localities require a specific number of work search activities per week in order to receive unemployment insurance benefits. This provides one guideline to assess the Plaintiff's job search diligence.

Additionally, a sufficiently diligent job search is that the job seeker will put an appropriate amount of time into their job search. The amount of time required for a sufficient job search of course also varies and depends on the Plaintiffs individual characteristics and the labor market. However, some general guidelines regarding the time that individuals spend on a typical job search can be obtained from publicly available labor market data published by the U.S. Bureau of Labor Statistics.

(Deposition testimony excerpt, wrongful termination Plaintiff with a Bachelor's degree)

Q: How many hours a week do you spend looking for jobs, for employment?
A: I would say approximately two hours on Internet searches.
Q: Per week?
A: That's correct.

The Plaintiff's testimony in this case regarding the time spent on the job search is actually very consistent with that of a typical job searcher. BLS data indicates that individuals who are looking for employment spend upward of two hours a day on average searching for employment. The job search activities that these individuals undertake include internet searches, networking with colleagues, placing applications, and interviewing. In addition, this data shows that individuals who are looking for employment and have higher levels of education and those with more specialized jobs tend to spend more time in a given week on job search activities. Individuals with more job experience and time in the labor market also tend to spend more time on job searching.

More specifically, the BLS data shows that job search time tends to increase significantly as the individual's education level increases. For instance, individuals looking for employment who have a High School diploma spend an average of 2.13 hours a day on job search related activities. In contrast, individuals who have an advanced degree spend more than 3.2 hours more each day searching for employment. The additional job search time for individuals with higher levels of educational attainment is due to a number of factors. Individuals with more education generally take a longer period of time to search for and find a job that is a good fit with their knowledge and experience. Interviews for these types of job positions that require advanced degrees also typically last longer than interviews for a lower level position. The types of positions that require advanced degrees generally require multiple interview sessions with various members of the company's executives.

Similar to education level, individuals who hold jobs that require specialized skills or training may find that their job position is more in demand and spend less time on job search. For example, occupations such as Emergency Medical Technicians (EMTs) and Paramedics require additional educational programs in order to obtain employment. EMT's and Paramedics are typically required to have a high school diploma or equivalent and cardiopulmonary resuscitation (CPR) certification to enter into these programs. Most programs are nondegree award programs, but some paramedics may need an associates degree. EMTs and Paramedics typically require state certification. Data shows that EMT's and Paramedics experience lower unemployment rates and job search times than other occupations with the same educational attainment.

Similarly, Heavy Truck Drivers require additional credentials than a typical worker. Individuals working as Heavy Truck Drivers may attend a professional truck driving school and must have a commercial driver's license (CDL). Unemployment rates and job search times for Heavy Truck Drivers, requiring nondegree awards, are less than that for individuals in other occupations with the same educational requirements. In addition to education, the amount of time an individual could be expected to search for a job is also dependent on experience level. Data from the BLS shows that the amount of time spent job searching generally increases as an individual's level of work experience increases.

A Comparison of Job Search Efforts for Identical Plaintiffs

	Plaintiff A	*Plaintiff B*
Begin of Job search	Two days following employment termination	Three weeks following employment termination
Average Job Search Activities per Week	Six per week on average	One or less on average per week
Variation in Job Application Rate	At least three job search activities per week in each of last eight weeks	Vast majority of job search activities (approx. 80%) were clustered in two weeks; most weeks in last eight weeks had no job search activity

The above example shows the post-termination work search of two Plaintiffs. Both Plaintiffs are identical and were looking for replacement employment in the same geographic area. Both Plaintiffs have currently spent eight weeks on their replacement employment search.

Plaintiff A shown on the left panel illustrates a consistent job search performed by the Plaintiff. Plaintiff A began their job search essentially immediately upon the end of their employment with the Defendant; whereas Plaintiff B waited a period of time before beginning their job search. Further, Plaintiff A conducted a thorough and consistent job search during the reported period of unemployment. Plaintiff A applied for an average of six jobs per week, while Plaintiff B had an average job application per week less than one. It is also clear from the job search that Plaintiff A was consistently searching for employment and applying for jobs evenly through the period of unemployment. Plaintiff B's applications were heavily clustered in two weeks of the period of unemployment.

More formally, a third characteristic of a diligent job search is that the Plaintiff's job search activities will be consistent over time and will commence relatively soon, if not before, the employment ended with the defendant employer. Typically, job searches will be most successful when started early. Industry or market connections still remain in place when the individual first leaves the job. It is typical to find employment through word of mouth between other individuals that are still connected to the industry and potential job opportunities. These connections are most important for individuals that are firmly rooted in their occupation at the time of their search.

Employers also may provide employees with access to industry organizations for networking that individuals may be able to utilize to obtain replacement employment. Access to those industry organization job boards and contacts are essential in providing opportunities and connections that allow the Plaintiff to obtain replacement employment in a reasonable period of time.

In addition to making the Plaintiff's job search more efficient and effective, job searches that occur relatively soon following their employment termination, also help lessen the likelihood of having long gaps between employment. A number of labor market studies and surveys have shown the impact of having large gaps of unemployment on the hiring process. These studies tend to show that long gaps in employment serve as caution flags for employers, especially if there is not a reasonable explanation for the candidate's workforce absence.

Below is an excerpt from the Plaintiff's deposition describing his job search post-termination.

Q: Have you limited your job search to Austin?
A: No. Because many of the jobs I've applied for are either worldwide or national jobs based on my experience, so many jobs require travel and I'm quite willing to do that.

In this example, the Plaintiff in this matter adjusted his job search to fit the type of job position he was looking to obtain following the termination of his employment with the defendant employer. The Plaintiff's job search expansion is consistent with a diligent job search.

Specifically, as described above, a diligent job search will be sufficiently geographically expansive. Depending on the particular job position, the labor market and the employer demand may be city wide, regional, statewide, or national for the Plaintiff's knowledge, skills and abilities. For a number of jobs, especially jobs that are performed online and require relatively little face to face interaction, employer demand can be national in scope. Alternatively, some specialized job positions, where the individual employee has obtained very specialized knowledge, may be somewhat more geographically limited.

In practice, the Plaintiff's job search records and the geographic distribution of their job search activity provides a good starting point for determining the scope of a Plaintiff's labor market. That is, examining the location of the Plaintiff's job search activity is a way to define the relevant job market to analyze. It is reasonable to assume that a job seeker would apply for job positions in locations that have sufficient employer demand for their skill sets and that they would apply for employment in geographical areas that they are willing to live in or move to to obtain employment.

In a case involving the termination of an employee in a Worldwide Sales Lead position, the Plaintiff's job search was geographically broad and reflected the nature of his position. The Plaintiff, prior to his termination, lived in Austin, Texas but spent most of his time outside of the Austin, Texas area. The Plaintiff's job position required him to frequently travel for work in his sales position.

In addition to being geographically broad, a diligent replacement job search will be occupationally broad. That is, the Plaintiff will tend to look for not only the same job that they held at the time of their employment termination, but will also seek employment in jobs that are related, and demand a similar skill set as the one they previously held. The qualifications and skill sets that a job seeker has is not typically limited to only one job and the person could apply to many different job positions in different industries. Labor market data resources like the BLS Occupational Outlook Handbook (OOH) are helpful and provide insights on the knowledge, skill and experience requirements of the Plaintiff's job position and also identifies job positions that are related to the one that is at issue in a case.

The following case illustrates the use of the OOH labor market data to assess the job market for a Plaintiff. In this case in Federal Court, the Plaintiff worked as a Bank Teller when her employment ended. The Plaintiff stated that she had been unemployed for over a year and a half and had not been able to obtain replacement employment. The Plaintiff testified that she had only looked for and applied for bank teller positions during the time after her employment ended with the defendant employer.

From a labor market standpoint, the Plaintiff's job search is not consistent with a person who is diligently attempting to obtain replacement employment. The Plaintiff in this instance was a bank teller with a job that has skills that are transferable to any number of different occupations with employers in various industries. For instance, bank tellers routinely interface with consumers and assist them with various services as well as resolve customer problems. These types of job responsibilities are required in numerous job positions such as customer service representatives, in many different industries. According to the BLS OOH, bank tellers have similar job responsibilities as jobs such as Auditing Clerks, Customer Services Representatives, and Information Clerks. It is reasonable to expect that a person who is diligently searching for replacement employment will consider these types of related jobs in addition to the job position of bank teller.

Finally, a job seeker that is diligently seeking employment would be expected to use all of the job search resources they have available to find a job. These resources may be in the form of job search programs, application assistance, network connections, or offers for employment. In practice it is expected that a diligently searching Plaintiff will utilize all that is available.

In a case involving a high level employee, at the time of her termination she was offered to participate in a job search program for executives. The job search program offered the Plaintiff an initial coaching session, resume preparation, interview and networking skills coaching, career and job search coaching, customized job leads, career assessments, access to online programs, and job offer negotiation coaching. The Plaintiff did not take advantage of the program offered to her and did not find comparable replacement employment. An analysis of the job market and the Plaintiff's job search revealed that she did not participate in a thorough job search. The programs offered by the employer, that the Plaintiff did not take advantage of, could have provided her with guidance and additional replacement job opportunities.

An individual diligently seeking work and attempting to mitigate their damages would be expected to accept a reasonable job offer for employment. A number of state workforce agencies actually require individuals who are receiving unemployment benefits to accept a reasonable job offer. For example, some state agencies require a recipient to be willing to accept a suitable job that pays at least 90% of their normal wage during the first eight weeks of unemployment. After a recipient has been unemployed for eight weeks, they must be willing to accept a suitable job that pays at least 75% of their normal wage. The percentages of course vary by state agency.

The Plaintiff's job search records and other related items obtained during discovery can provide useful insight into the effort that was made to obtain replacement employment. Deposition testimony can also provide additional information and insights. The following deposition excerpt is from a wrongful termination case involving a bank manager.

(Deposition excerpt from wrongful termination case involving a bank manager)

> Q: So let's talk about your job search after you left [the defendant-employer]. What did you do to look for work?
> A: Well, I started searching for jobs through Indeed or any of the employment websites, went to specific company websites.
> Q: What type of job were you looking for?
> A: Lending; jobs where I felt I would -- I qualified for.
> Q: What other types of jobs outside of lending did you apply for?
> A: There were several but each of them that I applied for were managerial, administrative, call center and or customer service related.
> Q: And you said you used a job site called Indeed and other employment websites?
> A: Yes, also LinkedIn.
> Q: Now in terms of your effort to look for work, I understand that you received your real estate license after you were terminated, correct?
> A: Yes, ma'am.
> Q: Have you continued a job search of any sort since you obtained your real estate license?

A: Yes, ma'am.
Q: And what has your job search consisted of after you obtained your real estate license?
A: Similar. I mean, my search hasn't changed with regards to the types of position that I'm seeking. I have extended it obviously outside of the city and even outside of the state.
Q: Has your effort in your job search diminished over time? For example, did you apply more applications before working in real estate versus now or since you've started working in real estate?
A: I'd say more selective. More lending, more loan related, and on my years of experience.
Q: What head hunters did you use?
A: I have them listed on my documents.
Q: Did you get any interest for applications you submitted?
A: Yes, I got interest from a credit union out of Florida. I got one out of Indiana. I got one out of Texas. I had two out of California. That's it.
Q: And let's talk about each of those. With the Florida credit union, how did they express interest? Did they ask you for an interview?
A: Through a head hunter.
Q: Did you get an offer?
A: No.
Q: And out of Indiana -- what happened with that application process?
A: I flew up there for an interview.
Q: Did an offer result?
A: No.
Q: Did offers result from any of these opportunities? From any of your job search efforts?
A: No.
Q: So of all the jobs you've applied for since your termination in this lawsuit, you didn't receive any job offers?
A: No.
Q: And did you get any feedback as to why you weren't considered or didn't receive an offer?
A: They didn't provide me with that. I did ask. I did inquire.
Q: Have your head hunters given you any feedback about why you may not be successful?
A: Any feedback they've given me has been very vague. So no, not anything that's been helpful.

Measuring Individualized Employer Demand

Abstract In this chapter, the other side of the labor market, that is labor demand by employers is discussed. In particular, we will discuss the data, methods, and measurement of the individual employer demand that Plaintiff encountered post-employment termination from the Defendant. An important portion of a labor market analysis is to determine what kind of employer demand exists for the Plaintiffs skill set and expertise. The employer demand for the Plaintiff's skills and expertise will help determine factors such as the expected post-termination salary and a reasonable post-employment termination job search time. There are multiple phases to a labor market analysis.

Keywords Labor market · Universe of employers · Direct/Indirect job openings · Unemployment duration · Underemployment

In the previous chapter, the Plaintiff's post-employment job search activities and essentially their willingness to supply their time and efforts to the labor market, i.e. labor supply, were discussed. In this chapter, the other side of the labor market, that is labor demand by employers is discussed. In particular, we will discuss the data, methods, and measurement of the individual employer demand that Plaintiff encountered post-employment termination from the Defendant.

The employer demand for the Plaintiff's skills and expertise is a key component in a post-employment termination labor market analysis. In some instances, the Plaintiff may face a post-employment termination labor market where there are a number of employers, and multiple job opportunities, vying for their skills in expertise. In other instances, the employer demand may not be as robust and/or there may be a relatively high number of job candidates vying for each job opportunity.

An important portion of a labor market analysis is to determine what kind of employer demand exists for the Plaintiffs skill set and expertise. The employer demand for the Plaintiff's skills and expertise will help determine factors such as the expected post-termination salary and a reasonable post-employment termination job search time. There are multiple phases to a labor market analysis.

Employer Demand Measurement Methodology

The first step is to determine the **universe of employers** who are hiring individuals with the Plaintiff's expertise, skill set and work history. The determination of the universe of hiring employers is generally made using information from publicly available labor market data sources and information provided by the Plaintiff during discovery. Publicly available data such as nation and state level job openings data, electronic job board postings, unemployment rate data, and local commerce reports such as those published by local Chambers of Commerce. Information obtained during the discovery process, such as the Plaintiffs job search emails, job search logs and Plaintiff deposition testimony can be useful in determining the universe of hiring employers. The case studies presented later in this book provide a number of examples of how this type of information is used in actual labor market analyses.

The second step is to **determine how many openings** that there are in the Plaintiff's occupational area. For instance, a registered nurse could be employed by a number of different employers, such as hospitals, clinics, medical testing facilities, nursing homes, and schools. Accordingly the demand for the appropriate universe of employers, and the number of job openings for these employers, should potentially be considered. In general, both direct and indirect job openings data is utilized in this stage of a labor market analysis.

Direct job openings data is data that is generated by the employer. Direct job openings data include data such as electronic job postings, such as those on Indeed.com, job placement agency database listings, want ads, and job fair job listings. These types of data are generally assembled by collecting data from state and local workforce agencies and various job posting websites. Most of these sources maintain current listings and a limited amount of historical job posting data. As will be discussed later in this chapter, historical data on job openings is available from a number of publicly available sources. The historical job openings data from these sources is generally available at a more aggregated occupational level.

The Job Conference Board produces The Help Wanted Online Data Series (HWOL) provides monthly measures of labor demand at the national, regional, state, and metropolitan area levels. The HWOL database provides the number of job openings for specific occupations that were available during a period of time in the various workforce development area locations.

Many states, such as Texas, Illinois, California, and Alabama utilize the HWOL system for state specific labor market information to publish on state workforce sites. The HWOL utilized by the Texas Workforce Commission also provides the percentage change in openings that position has experienced over the time period. Job opening data is generally available for the occupations classified by the Bureau of Labor Statistics. The HWOL data presented by the different state agencies may provide additional information. For instance, the HWOL utilized by the Illinois Department of Employment Security also presents the employers with the greatest number of job postings in addition to standard information about job openings by region.

State-wide resources can be utilized as well as electronic job boards. Real time current job postings are available on many state Workforce Development boards and can be narrowed by job title and location. Current job openings can also be found through electronic job boards such as Indeed.com, Glassdoor.com, and SimplyHired.com. Job boards further allow for limiting filters when performing a job search such as location mileage range, salary, job type, experience level, and other specific factors that may apply to the Plaintiff's labor market..

Indirect job openings data is information that is gleaned from the tabulation and analysis of various direct labor market data sources. For instance, the unemployment rate within the Plaintiff's occupation is a frequently relied upon source of indirect data on job openings.

In general, occupations with a high number of job seekers relative to employer demand will see higher unemployment rates in those positions. Conversely, occupations with lower unemployment rates, all other factors being equal, are suggestive of an occupation where there are a smaller number of job seekers relative to the employer demand for those job positions.

While job level unemployment rates are useful in the study of job seekers in the Plaintiff's relevant occupation, there are a number of factors that should be considered when analyzing the relative unemployment rates in the Plaintiff's occupational areas. For instance, the natural unemployment rate of the Plaintiff's occupational area needs to be taken into account in the analysis. In some industries, such as the oil and gas industry, employment opportunities are highly correlated to the price of the underlying product or commodity. Accordingly, the unemployment rate for individuals in occupations heavily concentrated in these types of industries may be more volatile than other occupations that are not as concentrated in such industries. Additionally, some occupations where employee turnover is relatively high, such as those in some service and production jobs, typically have higher unemployment rates than the national average. Unemployment rates also tend to be correlated with demographic factors such as educational attainment, workforce training levels, and work experience.

The third step is to **determine how long** it should reasonably take an individual who is diligently searching to find replacement employment. In many instances, the analysis involves and focuses on the individual Plaintiff finding employment that was comparable to the one that is at issue in the employment lawsuit. While the determination of if a job is comparable is often a legal issue in the case, the issue of comparability is more clear and less controversial from a labor market perspective. As was discussed in the previous chapters and in the case studies provided in this text, comparability of the Plaintiff's occupation to occupations can be assessed by examining the key components of the Plaintiff's occupation. Sources such as the BLS Occupational handbook are used to determine the comparability of the Plaintiff's occupation to that of other occupations.

As for measuring the expected job search time, publicly available labor data, and when available, occupation specific data, is generally used to analyze this issue. One frequently utilized method is to use micro level and person specific BLS data on unemployment duration at the occupation level. This data can be used to measure how long an individual who is actively in the labor market and similarly situated to the Plaintiff, took to find replacement employment following the cessation of their previous employment. This data can be used to focus on individuals with similar educational backgrounds, geographical locations, and other relevant factors.

The fourth step is to **determine the salary and compensation** that a diligently job searching Plaintiff could expect from comparable employment. Compensation data, depending on the individual's occupation, can be obtained from publicly available sources such as BLS as well as privately maintained sources such as those assembled by electronic job boards and professional support organizations. Electronic job posting sites such as Glassdoor, Indeed.com are also prime sources of compensation information and are generally accepted and utilized in compensation analysis.

Additional benefits data can be obtained from sites such as Salary.com. The data on salary.com and some similar sites allows a deep dive into the typical benefits packages for a given occupation. Further benefits details provided include items such as average bonus amount, retirement benefits, and typical vacation and time off benefits.

State agency workforce commission data can also be useful in the analysis of the Plaintiff's salary and compensation. Most states maintain labor market data on salary, compensation, employment projects, and the job openings. The state agency data generally provides annual and hourly wage estimates for various occupations by state, metropolitan and workforce development area, and industry. These tools can provide information regarding mean and median wages, entry level wages, experienced wages, and additional percentile increments.

Plaintiff's Expected Unemployment Duration

So how long should it take a diligently searching Plaintiff to find comparable replacement employment? In employment termination cases, that is an important question that needs to be addressed when calculating alleged back pay and front losses. Unlike other types of torts involving individuals, such as injury cases, able bodied Plaintiffs in employment litigation are capable of obtaining replacement employment and if they are diligent to the job search process they should be able to regain employment within a reasonable period of time. Determining the reasonable period of job search time for the Plaintiff assists the trier of facts in the assessment of an appropriate back and front pay loss time period.

Data on a reasonable period of job search time can be obtained from the U.S. Bureau of Labor Statistics. The BLS publishes tabulations of unemployment rates for individuals in various industries, and geographic areas. The BLS also releases publicly available individual, person level data that can be used to calculate more detailed unemployment durations for specific occupations and by different demographics such as the age of the individual.

So what does the BLS unemployment duration data say about how long is reasonable for a diligent job search? The BLS unemployment duration and job search data provides several overarching themes. One, the unemployment duration data indicates that unemployment durations over a year for most occupations and individuals diligently searching for replacement employment are unlikely. For instance, in 2018 the average unemployment duration and job search time was 21.21 weeks which is of course significantly less than a year. Overall, out of the 448 occupations in the 2018 BLS data, 270, or 60.3%, of them had average unemployment durations that were less than 21.21 weeks. More than 96% of the occupations had average unemployment durations and job search times that were less than one year.

Two, the BLS unemployment duration data also shows that job search time for a diligent individual looking for replacement employment varies across different geographic regions. For example, the average job search time in the state of Iowa was approximately 14.2 weeks. In comparison, the average job search time for individuals in the District of Columbia was approximately 35.4 weeks.

Three, in addition, the BLS unemployment rate and job search data indicates that an individual's education level will also have an impact on the time that can reasonably be expected to take to find replacement employment. Overall, individuals with higher levels of education experience significantly lower rates of unemployment but the job search time for these individuals tends to be higher than those with lower levels of education attainment. Specifically, the unemployment rate falls as the educational attainment of the individual increases. For instance, over the last five years, the unemployment rate for an individual with a Bachelor's degree was less than half that of individuals with a High School Diploma.

Conversely, the job search time for individuals with higher levels of education tends to be longer for persons with higher levels of education. For instance, over the last five year, the average job search time for individuals with a post-Bachelor's advanced degree is over 2.1 weeks longer than for individuals with a High School diploma.

Fourth, individuals with higher salaries tend to take longer to find replacement employment than those with lower salaries. For instance, in the most recent year an individual in Business and Financial Operations occupations with an average salary of approximately $50,000 had an average job search time of 17.8 weeks. In comparison, individuals in Business and Financial Operations occupations with an average salary of approximately $100,000 had an average job search and unemployment duration of 26.7 weeks.

UNDEREMPLOYMENT AND RETIREMENT

In some instances, the Plaintiff will obtain replacement employment rather quickly, if not immediately, after their employment is terminated with the Defendant. However, in some of these cases, the job position that the individual obtained was not in line with their work history and experience. In some of these instances, the individual is what is referred to as underemployed. Underemployment is the underuse of a worker because a job does not fully utilize the worker's skills, is part-time, or is otherwise inconsistent with the individual document work history and experience.

An example of an underemployed Plaintiff is shown below.

Requirements of Plaintiff's Job Position while employed with Defendant	*Requirements of Plaintiff's Replacement Employment*
• Four year college degree from accredited university required	• High school degree required
• Requiring 5 years of experience; plus 2 years in a managerial role	• 0–1 years of experience
• $62,300 annual salary	• $16.50 per hour, working on an as needed basis; averages 25 hours per week
• Benefits include health insurance, retirement contributions, and annual bonuses	• Offers health insurance to employees

The Plaintiff in the example above could be considered underemployed.

Other factors to consider in terms of re-employment opportunities are the typical retirement age. Some occupations for example have average retirement ages that are significantly lower than the average overall. For example, police officers and firefighters tend to have earlier retirement ages on average than other occupations. The impact of a Plaintiff's middle and later year changes is also a factor that may be important to the person's re-employment opportunities.

Interest Rate Discounting Front Pay Losses

Abstract The third portion of the economic damage calculation in an employment termination case generally involves determining the present value of any future front pay losses. The process of interest rate discounting is not controversial and involves a straightforward arithmetic calculation. This chapter discusses interest rate discounting of back and front pay losses.

Keywords Time value of money · Present value · Interest rate · Discount factor · Future income

The third portion of the economic damage calculation in an employment termination case generally involves determining the present value of any future front pay losses. The process of interest rate discounting is not controversial and involves a straightforward arithmetic calculation. This chapter discusses interest rate discounting of back and front pay losses.

Present Value and Interest Rate Discounting

Conceptually, the present value calculation involves determining how much money would have to be deposited in a relatively safe investment today to compensate the Plaintiff for the dollar income losses that the Plaintiff is expected to experience over the relevant portions of the person's work life. The amount to be deposited in a safe investment, such as a U.S. treasury security, is called the present value of the future stream of income. The underlying premise in the present value calculation is that a dollar received tomorrow, at the time that the person actually experiences the alleged loss, is worth less than a dollar received today. A dollar received tomorrow is worth less today because a dollar received today can be invested, or deposited in a bank account today that will earn interest, until the time the money is needed.

In the calculation, the present value of any alleged future losses takes into accounts what is referred to as the 'time value of money'. The underlying time value of money premise in the present value calculation is that a dollar received tomorrow is worth less than a dollar received today. This is because a dollar received today can be invested, or deposited in a bank account today that will earn interest and grow until the time the money is actually needed at the later date. Conversely, if the person receives a dollar tomorrow, or at a later date, they will not have the opportunity to earn interest on that money that they receive at the later date.

To illustrate the concept of the present value of money, consider an example of an employment lawsuit in which a 62-year-old Plaintiff whose employment was allegedly wrongfully terminated. Assume, for the purposes of this example, that there is no issue of liability and the defendant is simply attempting to calculate the total value of the economic damages. Further, assume both sides have agreed that the terminated employee lost $50,000 per year at the time of his termination and will continue to lose that amount each year until retirement at the age of 65.

One way to determine the economic value of the lost wages in this example would be simply to multiply the amount the person was earning at the time of his employment by three years, which would mean that the defendant has caused a total of $150,000 in economic damages to the Plaintiff. This simplistic calculation is, of course, incorrect because the Plaintiff's loss of income does not all incur today. Instead, the Plaintiffs losses actually would occur in the future over the next three years.

Accordingly, conceptually the Plaintiff could take a lesser amount today, put it into a bank account or other safe investment, and with interest they have the amount of money that they will need at the future point. The amount that the Plaintiff will need today to have the future needed amount, is called the present value. If as described above, a lump sum equal to the whole undiscounted amount of the loss was awarded, the Plaintiff would receive a windfall, since with interest, an undiscounted lump sum award would result in an amount greater than the amount needed to replace the lost future income.

The process of discounting requires a projection as to how much interest the lump sum award would earn. This is a key projection because the present value of the lump sum award is inversely related to the interest rate discount factor. That is the present value of the lump sum award increases as the interest rate discount factor decreases. Conversely, the higher the assumed interest rate discount, the smaller the present value of the lump sum.

Example Calculation

For example, a present value interest rate discount factor of 5% will yield a lower value than a present value interest discount factor of 1%. When interest rates are higher, i.e. 5% in the example, the amount of interest that is foregone by not receiving the money today is greater, therefore the present value of the alleged future losses is lower. In other words, when interest rates are higher, the Plaintiff could earn higher rates of interest on money invested today so they will need to have less money today to grow to meet the future loss. Conversely, and for the same reasons, a lower present value interest rate discount factor results in a higher value for the Plaintiff's future alleged losses. In this situation, when interest rates are lower, the Plaintiff will earn lower rates of interest on money invested today so they will need to have more money today to grow to meet the future loss.

In employment termination calculations, it is generally accepted to utilize a relatively low interest rate. All things being considered equal, higher interest rates, such as those that could be expected from investing in a company's stock, reflect underlying market factors including risk. Accordingly, a relatively low interest rate reflects a relatively low level of underlying risk. Conceptually an interest rate such as one based on investment returns could be utilized but is not typically done in practice.

Utilization of an interest discount factor that is based on stock market returns would require the Plaintiff to be able to make investments in relatively risky assets that on average return a higher than average rate of return than a safe investment such as a U.S. Treasury.

In most employment cases involving individuals that are classified as employees, the present day value of the Plaintiff's alleged economic damages in employment cases is typically calculated using interest rate data from safe investments such as U.S. Treasury Bills, Bonds, and Notes. A safe investment such as U.S. Treasuries for the most part will return the stated rate of return without requiring the Plaintiff to have specialized knowledge of financial markets or being able to time assets purchases and sells. The idea is that the Plaintiff should not be required to be a sophisticated investor in the calculation of the present value. In some cases, a safe rate such as the U.S. Treasury is not appropriate. In some instances such as where the Plaintiff's compensation at the defendant-employer is variable or is tied to the employer's company profits, a higher interest rate discount rate may be appropriate.

Table 1 provides an example of a present value calculation. The table assumes that the Plaintiff is able to obtain a safe interest rate of return of 5.0% per year. The table shows how much the Plaintiff would need to be compensated for front pay losses that occur into the future. For instance, assuming an interest rate discount factor of 5.0%, the Plaintiff would need $47,619 to compensate them for a loss that would be incurred one year into the future. Put differently, the Plaintiff could place $47,619 in an

Table 1 The present value of Plaintiff's front pay losses

Year of front pay loss	Plaintiff's front pay loss	How much does the Plaintiff need today to replace the Plaintiff's future front pay loss?
1 Year into future	$50,000	$47,619
2 Year into future	$50,000	$45,351
3 Year into future	$50,000	$43,192
Total Plaintiff undiscounted front pay loss	$150,000	
Total discounted present value of Plaintiff's front pay losses incurred one to three years into the future		$136,162

account that paid 5.0% per year and that would give the individual the $50,000 that would be needed at the end of year one.

Similarly, the Plaintiff would need $45,351 to replace the $50,000 loss that is projected to occur two years into the future. The amount is less because the Plaintiff would have an additional year of interest, so less money is needed today to be placed into the bank account paying 5.0% interest. The Plaintiff would need a total of $136,162 to be invested in the bank account paying 5.0% to replace a three year total loss of $150,000.

In addition to the interest rate discount factor, a number of other factors need to be considered. These include the Plaintiff's future salary growth, the Plaintiff's expected job tenure with the Defendant, job turnover trends, and outside employer demand for the Plaintiffs' job experience and skills.

Insights from Labor Market Research and Data

Abstract A Plaintiff's ability to regain comparable replacement employment is a critical component when calculating back and front pay damages. The construction of such analyses rely on crucial economic concepts, data, and labor market research. This chapter discusses various considerations that contribute to a Plaintiff's mitigation analysis such as post-termination employment, job search behavior, job tenure, available job openings, and job evaluations, and includes useful labor data sources.

Keywords Post-termination employment · Duration of unemployment · Work life · Job tenure · Job evaluations

A Plaintiff's ability to regain comparable replacement employment is a critical component when calculating back and front pay damages. The construction of such analyses rely on crucial economic concepts, data, and labor market research.

Job Search and Mitigation Labor Market Research

Franz in *Wrongful Employment Termination and Resulting Economic Losses* (1990) sets out critical assumptions that should be considered in

© The Author(s), under exclusive license to Springer Nature Switzerland AG 2022
D. Steward, *Economic Losses and Mitigation after an Employment Termination*,
https://doi.org/10.1007/978-3-030-88364-5_6

calculations of back pay and future earnings. Franz notes that, in a legal setting, employees have an obligation to mitigate their damages, such as demonstrating a reasonable effort in finding new employment that is substantively equivalent to their prior jobs. Those attempting to calculate damages have to consider, for example, the present value of earnings from alternate employment, which in turn have to be adjusted for the costs to find an alternative job (like time). Since this seminal work, economists and forensic economists have refined mitigation analyses with new research and data, particularly in the realm of job searches and post-termination employment.

For example, if a Plaintiff is still able to work post-termination, it is generally accepted that their damages should end at some reasonable period of time. The data and economic literature show, by contrast, that able bodied employees are readily able to find jobs after separation. How long it takes for an employee to find a job after separation depends, of course, on demographic and occupational differences, but the concept remains the same. Rather than relying on conjecture, assumptions in employment termination analyses are founded on principles derived from key economic literature.

The literature and data on employment separation or termination is extensive, but points to the conclusion that able-bodied employees can readily find employment after a previous position.

There are a variety of different data sources that can be used to analyze a Plaintiff's job search efforts. For example, the Bureau of Labor Statistics' Current Population Survey (CPS) measures how many weeks the unemployed search for replacement work until they are hired into a new position (or drop out of the labor force). This is called the "Duration of Unemployment." In 2019, a U.S. job seeker, on average, about 20–25 weeks unemployed before they found a new job. The average number of weeks of unemployment has varied substantially in the past ten years: post-2008 the average time a U.S. worker was unemployed peaked at 40 weeks, and then steadily declined over the next decade. Spells of unemployment that last more than a year are relatively rare for the typical U.S. job seeker who is diligently seeking replacement employment.

When a worker does become unemployed, the intensity of their job search, measured along metrics like the number of minutes per day they spend seeking work, or the number of job applications they submit per day or week, are important metrics. In a litigation setting, a less intense job search by the Plaintiff signals effort to find replacement employment.

There are a number of sources which measure how much time Americans spend searching for jobs, such as the American Time Use Survey or the Current Population Survey. A listing and description of some commonly utilized labor market databases is provided at the end of this chapter.

Job search intensity varies depending on demographic factors like age or gender. Knowing these factors further refines a mitigation analysis by comparing the Plaintiff's job search to their peers. In the 2013 paper titled *The Life-Cycle Profile of Time Spent on Job Search* by Aguilar, Hurst, and Karabarbounis, the authors discovered that older unemployed workers spend far more time searching for jobs than younger unemployed workers. The paper utilized information from the American Time Use Survey (ATUS). Job seekers aged 46–55 spent, on average 6.6 hours a week job searching, while job seekers aged 21–25 spent on average 2.2 hours a week job searching. Men, on average, spent an additional 2.3 hours a week job searching compared to women.

The advent of online job search websites has led to shorter spells of unemployment, as demonstrated by a Faberman and Kudlayk paper titled *The Intensity of Job Search and Search Duration*. Utilizing information from an online job search site, the authors found that the average unemployed worker spends about 30 minutes per day searching for work, for between 5 to 6 weeks. The exact amount of time spent per day searching for work varies by demographic cohorts, but most job seekers spend 3.5 hours searching per week. In about 5 to 6 weeks, the average job seeker was able to finish their job search.

Individual job search efforts decline over time, meaning that people submit more applications within the first few weeks of unemployment than later weeks. The authors concluded that job seekers who search more intensely tend to be older, male, and tend to have separated from long-tenured jobs. However, online job search sites are much more pervasive than in previous years, and given the low cost (to job seekers), their effectiveness in finding work has decreased job search times.

Finally, job search behavior can depend on broader economic conditions. Job seekers spend more time searching for work when economic conditions appear depressed. This phenomenon was identified in a 2018 paper by Mukoyama, Patterson, and Sahin titled *Job Search Behavior over the Business Cycle*. The authors found that, between 2008 and 2014, job seekers increased the amount of time they spent searching for work, compared to the pre-2008 period. Indeed, job search intensity seemed to increase as unemployment increased.

Unemployment durations and job search efforts remain two critical components of any mitigation analysis. Both the data and research point to the conclusion that damages do not extend infinitely into the future. Most U.S. workers are able to find another job within months, or weeks, of separation, and one key component of that ability is a worker's job search.

Most analyses also consider the relevant work life remaining of the employee. Plaintiffs may assert that they would live to retirement age, a statement that presumably everyone would wish to be true. However, based on previous research into life expectancy, an employee's departure from the workforce before retirement age, such as disability, death, or voluntary withdrawal, must be taken into account.

Job tenure is another factor that weighs heavily in a mitigation analysis. Plaintiffs may argue that, had they not been terminated, they would have continued in their current position or with their current employer indefinitely. This claim of a "career job" however, can be met with due skepticism based on available evidence from the research literature. The data suggests that most employees do not spend their entire lives working in a single job. Rather, employees tend to move between jobs after a few years.

In a 2015 paper titled *Employee Tenure Trends, 1983–2014*, author Craig Copeland demonstrates that "career jobs" are highly uncommon for U.S. employees. In fact, the average employee stays in a given job for about 5 years. Copeland did find that older employees had longer job tenure than younger employees. Still, even among those aged 55–64, the median job tenure U.S. employees was just over 10 years. Even after accounting for age differences, only about 30% of U.S. private sector employees stayed in the same job for 10 years or more, and only 5% of U.S. private-sector employees stayed in the same job for 25 years or more. This study is only one example demonstrating how few "career jobs" actually exist in the economy.

The Copeland study corroborated evidence provided in a 2010 chapter by Henry Farber titled *Job Loss and the Decline in Job Security in the United States* from the book, *Labor in the New Economy*, shows that about a third of private sector workers stayed in a job more than 10 years. Farber demonstrated that, by 2008, only 37% of male employees in the private sector stayed in a job for more than 10 years, and only 30% of female employees in the private sector stayed in a job for more than 10 years. Farber found that younger employees have a mean job tenure well under 10 years. Men and women aged 40 in the private sector, for example, had an average job tenure of between 6 and 8 years.

For forensic economics, the exploration of job turnover probabilities was captured most notably by Robert Trout in *Duration of Employment In Wrongful Termination Cases* (1995). Trout emphasized that a mitigation analysis has to seriously consider the likelihood that, but-for an alleged wrongful termination, the Plaintiff would have remained working with their employer up to retirement. Trout demonstrated, by using available Current Population Survey (CPS) data, this is very unlikely.

Trout models the probability that a given employee will remain in the same job in the next year as the year before, given the employee's income, age, education, and employer tenure. In Trout's calculations, it is less likely an employee will stay with a given employer several years into the future. This gradually increasing attrition rate has to be considered when calculating losses in a wrongful termination case.

Utilizing available CPS data, Trout shows that, historically, annual employee job turnover rates were approximately 10%. However, Trout noted that turnover rates vary across individual, job and industry characteristics; the more of these factors that are controlled for, the more reliable one's mitigation calculations.

Rather than relying on aggregate national data and statistics, if internal corporate data is available, a mitigation analysis can utilize information on attrition for similarly-situated employees. Building upon Trout's method, White, Tranfa-Abboud, and Holt construct a method which takes into account different attrition rates for employees across years and "levels" within a company. The author's paper, *The Use of Attrition Rates for Economic Loss Calculations in Employment Discrimination Cases: A Hypothetical Case Study* (2003) argues that not incorporating a Plaintiff's probability of their continued employment, utilizing the relevant corporate data, will likely lead to an overestimation of economic losses.

The authors emphasize that attrition data for employees similarly situated the Plaintiff will produce the most accurate estimates. For their purposes, similarly-situated employees are employees who possess similar qualifications and experience to the Plaintiff and who began employment or their career path at a similar point in time. The comparable attrition rate, therefore, is the number of employees in job "x" who left their employment during year "y," divided by the number of employees in job "x" who were still employed at the end of year "y-1." Such analysis should only consider employees who were terminated or who left voluntarily. The "retention rate" (1 - the attrition rate) thus gives a picture of how likely an employee would stay at the particular employer over time.

The authors suggest that factors such as education, training, prior experience, seniority, and the economic health of the firm should also be considered to refine such analysis. Once a mitigation analysis considers the retention rate at a firm, then the potential damages should be discounted to adjust for the likelihood that the Plaintiff will remain employed in that specific firm.

This literature was further synthesized by Charles Baum in a 2013 paper titled: *Employee Tenure and Economic Losses in Wrongful Termination Cases*. Baum develops a different model of employee retention and "job survival" by utilizing the National Longitudinal Survey of Youth (NLSY), which tracks a nationally representative sample of individuals beginning in 1979 through to the present. This sample includes the employment experiences of each participant. Baum argues that basing results on employer-specific tenure is critical because tenure is highly linked to retention rates. Rather than a static chance of quitting an employer (say a 5% chance every year), Baum's model allow this probability to adjust over time, given an employee's prior tenure at a firm.

Utilizing the NLSY data, Baum finds that many employment spells are relatively short, sometimes less than a year. Therefore, he argues that short tenures are associated with a high probability of leaving an employer. After a given length of time, as tenure increases, an employee has a higher probability of remaining with an employer (i.e. a lower attrition rate).

Baum finds, for example, that a slight majority of the employment spells do not last beyond the first year, in other words, almost half of employees do not remain with their employer after a signal year. He notes that, once an employee reaches, say, more than 10 years of employment, an employee has a less than 10% chance of ending their employment in years that follow. Baums concludes that many periods of employment do not last long, but those that do have a relatively low probability of ending in subsequent years. Baum also finds that attrition rates vary by factors such as gender.

Additionally, job churn or job turnover is another angle from which to study tenure in a given industry or occupation. Industries with higher turnover rates, more hires and separations, necessarily imply shorter tenure, on average, than Industries with lower turnover. Examining job flows could identify specific age groups and industries where employees have higher attrition rates. This was the kind of strategy employed by Abowd and Vihuber in a 2011 paper titled *National Estimates of Gross Employment and Job Flow, Quarterly Workforce Indicators with Demographic and Industry Detail.*

The authors found large differences in job turnover by age and an employee's industry. There were significantly higher job turnover among younger employees, than older employees. Employees aged 19–24, for example, had nearly four times the turnover rate of employees aged 55–64. The authors also found large industry differences in job churn. The Agricultural, Construction, Entertainment, and Accommodation industries had higher than average job turnover rates. Industries like Utilities, Manufacturing, and Finance had lower than average job turnover rates. The authors concluded that job turnover rates varied enormously by age group, and also by age group across industrial sectors.

The research points to significant changes in job tenure over the average employee's life, tenure which varies by age and industry. Older employees had longer job tenure compared to younger employees, making age an important factor to consider in an analysis. Job turnover also varies by industry, and is especially volatile in blue-collar and low-wage service sector industries. The research, however, shows that for most American employees, staying in a single job for an extended period of time is rare.

However, age alone cannot be considered in a vacuum. Mitigation analyses also have to consider when an employee, at a given age, is hired by a firm and if there are any firm specific effects.

To underline the practical implications of this subtle distinction, David Rosenbaum provides a specific example in *The Impact of Age on Employment Tenure: Results from an Employment Discrimination Case* (2001) in the Journal of Forensic Economics. Rosenbaum overviews a class action suit which alleged a company wrongfully discriminated against applicants over age 40. The damage calculations required estimating the amount of time members of the class would have been employed at this firm, absent the discrimination.

The employer in the case argued that there was, indeed, a link between age and job tenure, but in their experience it ran in the reverse: older employees would not have worked as long as younger employees.

Rosenbaum utilizes corporate-level information about current and previous employees to predict the relationship between age and tenure. For previous employees, company records indicate the date of hire and the date of termination; tenure is calculated as the number of weeks from hire to termination. For current employees, however, Rosenbaum's calculations were modified to specify tenure as a function of age.

Rosenbaum's results for the company showed that a 24 yr old employee, for example, would have an expected job tenure of 166 weeks. However, a 40 yr old employee would have an expected tenure of 129 weeks. Utilizing the definitions of the class, Rosenbaum grouped together employees aged 39 or younger, of which the average age was 29. A 29 yr old employee at the firm had a tenure of 153 weeks. By contrast, the average age at application for workers at or older than 40 was 47. A 47-year-old employee would have an expected tenure of 115 weeks, about 25% less than the comparable younger worker. Rosenbaum's method showed that calculations of damages would need to consider the difference in tenure between older and younger employees. It also demonstrated the continued usefulness of available company data.

Knowing how many job openings there are for a given type of job provides important detail to the depth and scope of a Plaintiff's post termination employment search. Given the various avenues to finding a new job, whether it is on online job boards, through recruiters, job fares, or personal connections, identifying the number of job openings for a given occupation or industry may not sound straightforward. Several sources which collect data on job openings or postings are readily used for academic researchers and are considered highly reliable.

One such source is the Job Openings and Labor Turnover Survey, or JOLTS, put out by the Bureau of Labor Statistics. JOLTS provides monthly estimates of job openings, hires, and separations, collecting information from a sample of approximately 16,000 non-farm employers every month across the United States. JOLTS data is published at the industry level. The U.S. Current Population Survey (CPS) is a monthly survey of households conducted by the Bureau of Census for the Bureau of Labor Statistics that looks at key demographic and labor force characteristics like employment, hours of work, and earnings. CPS data includes occupations. Combining JOLTS and CPS data together, one could reconstruct a data series that has job openings by occupation.

This is exactly the strategy employed, for example, by Hobijn and Perkowski in their 2016 paper: *The Industry-Occupation Mix of U.S. Job Openings and Hires*. The co-authors were interested in examining shifts in job vacancies since 2007 and the interplay between vacancies by occupation and the unemployment rate. In order to evaluate the data, the authors combined the available vacancy data from JOLTS and the occupational mix available in the CPS, using an employee's industry as a bridge between the data. The detailed findings and conclusion of the paper could be discussed at length. For example, the authors concluded that employees who lost their jobs in one sector of the economy were relatively able to find jobs in another sector, even another occupation (though not always at the same wages).

Of particular note however, is that the authors utilized publicly available data sets to evaluate how many job openings existed by occupation in a given industry, and could evaluate changes in openings over time. The authors constructed a method that allows non-academics, for example, to calculate vacancies in occupations in a given industry in a given region of the country.

Before the age of the internet, collecting information on all available job postings for a given region was difficult. With the rise of online job boards, collecting and publishing data on open jobs postings became easier. Websites and databases could more easily store and track trends in job postings by occupation. One source is the Help Wanted Online (HWOL) data published by The Conference Board. HWOL data aggregates all of the online job ads over 50,000 web sites publishing job openings in the United States. HWOL data includes job postings from large online domains like Glassdoor or Linkedin, to smaller web domains that serve niche occupations or regions in the United States.

Burning-Glass.com, is another prominent online source of online job postings. Burning Glass is a job market analytics firm which provides up to date information about labor market demands by analyzing hundreds of millions of job postings. Burning Glass asserts it has a database of over a billion historical job openings to track trends in employment and marketable skills at a national, state, or local level. The firm's data is open to partners and interested researchers. In 2015, The Conference Board and Burning Glass partnered to refine the HWOL index, which tracks monthly trends in the U.S. job market.

Online job postings data is a highly useful tool for researchers studying job market trends by specific occupations. A study released by the University of Georgetown titled *UNDERSTANDING ONLINE JOB ADS DATA*, by Carnevale, Jayasundera, and Repnikov, examined how representative online ads were for the broader labor market. The authors relied upon both HWOL and Burning Glass's databases of online advertisements. The authors found that between 60 and 70% of job openings are now posted on the internet, and that trends in the number of online job postings tracked well with vacancies reported by JOLTS. They also discovered that online job postings were skewed towards applicants with college degrees and white collar occupations. Jobs in sales, management, engineering, technology, and the sciences tended to comprise the majority of online job postings. The paper concluded that online job postings, if used carefully, could reduce unemployment spells by increasing job matching efficiency.

Similarly, a special report commissioned by several Federal Reserve Banks in 2015, titled Identifying Opportunity Occupations in the Nation's Largest Metropolitan Areas, also relied on online job postings to study blue collar jobs. The authors, Wardrip, Fee, Nelson, and Andreason, investigated the extent to which employers were offering jobs that did not require a four-year college degree. Defining these occupations as "opportunity occupations," the authors use job postings data for the 100 largest metropolitan areas in the United States from Burning Glass. Combining this data with other public data sources like the Occupational Employment Statistics (OES), the authors constructed a measure of how prevalent specific "opportunity occupations" were by metropolitan area. The authors found that between 20.3 to 27.4% of employment opportunities were for "opportunity occupations" such as Automotive Service Technicians, Registered Nurses, Tractor-Trailer Truck Drivers, Sales Representatives, or Construction Workers. Of particular interest from this paper is that, despite known biases of online ads towards white collar professions, the authors were able to identify blue collar occupations and develop metrics to identify how many job openings there were for occupations with fewer educational requirements.

Devising available job postings for given occupations is a task which is made easier by publicly available data and the emergence of online job boards. Whether for high level management or for unskilled positions, being able to identify open jobs is a critical component of analyzing job search activities post separation. The academic research demonstrates several reliable methods and sources.

The use of online job ads is itself now a subject of inquiry in Forensic Economics. Cohen and Steiner (2013) in, *Using Online Help-Wanted Advertising Data and Other Indicators to Assess Whether a Plaintiff's Job Search was Sufficient to Mitigate Damages*, argue that web-based job ads can be used successfully in employment mitigation cases by introducing a new measure for evaluating a Plaintiff's diligence of a job search in a local the labor market. Cohen and Steiner argue that the number of applications a Plaintiff made, given the total number of applications for other comparable jobs, is a strong indicator of the Plaintiff's attempt to mitigate damages.

Utilizing a commercially available database of online job postings, Cohen and Steiner construct a ratio, known as the 'Ad Rate', which is of the number of help wanted ads over the number of employed workers in the same occupational category, for a given labor market (like a city or metroplex). This figure was highly correlated with statistics like the hire rate from JOLTS (previously mentioned), and the unemployment rate for a given occupation.

This ratio is used as another indicator to estimate how difficult it would be for a worker to find a job in a particular labor market. If say, there were more advertisements per 100 employed Registered Nurses in a given city than other occupations, that would imply that the job prospects and job search for a Registered Nurse should be relatively easier in comparison to other jobs. The Cohen and Steiner model is just one method by which online advertisements are now playing a part in the wider discussion of job seeking for mitigation analyses.

Occasionally Plaintiffs have a unique job or occupation, making it difficult to directly compare the compensation at their prior job to their current employment or other private sector standards. Establishing a salary benchmark is important, and it is important to base this benchmark on different individual components of the job in question. Such an analysis is already common in Human Resource Management, and is known as a Job Evaluation.

A job evaluation is a process by which a company or organization assesses the monetary value of a given job, based on the various job skills and tasks of the position. The monetary value of these various job tasks are then aggregated to generate an overall salary. The Job Evaluation method is described in detail by Morgeson, Brannick, and Levine in their book *Job and Work Analysis Methods, Research, and Applications for Human Resource Management*.

The analysis begins by detailing various job duties an employee is expected to perform. Asking what tasks the jobholder does, how the jobholder conducts the tasks, and why the tasks are performed. For example, Christal and Weissmuller, in a 1988 paper titled *Job-task inventory analysis*, did a thorough analysis as to how job tasks can be collected and studied. Such research has been followed up in the last few decades to analyze job tasks in a more objective way (for example, Goffin & Woycheshin in *An Empirical Method of Determining Employee Competencies/KSAOs From Task-Based Job Analysis*, published in 2009).

Then this task, or duty list, can be refined to identify which duties an employee is being paid for (a compensable factor). The co authors then highlight several different ways in which a job evaluation can be conducted, such as ranking different job duties. A 1989 paper titled *Job analysis*, Spector, Brannick, and Coovert examined the reliability and validity of various job analysis ratings, and demonstrated that even subjective measurements of job duty importance are reliable.

An objective job evaluation can be provided by using a statistical approach based on the market value of individual job tasks or skills.

The statistical approach creates a benchmark based on weighting the job tasks and a set of comparator jobs. Each job task has a relative weight in comparison to the total job. For example, Job Task 1 comprises 20% of the total job duties. The comparator jobs are comprised of duties that are a comparator to the specific job task. The salaries of this comparator job are multiplied by the weight of the job task it is being compared to. This is done for every job task and comparator job, with the final sum being the estimated salary for the position.

As the co authors note, a job evaluation requires information about a job that is comparable to other jobs, such as job tasks or skills. A job evaluation also requires some metric to translate job skills and tasks into a value. Job evaluation methods, which create benchmarks to compare jobs, are an invaluable tool when direct salary comparisons are impossible.

Useful Labor Data Sources

American Community Survey. The American Community Survey (ACS) is an annual survey of American households and individuals that gathers demographic information across the United States. Beginning in 2005, the survey randomly samples 1% of the American population every year (approximately 3.5 million people), to revise and update estimates gathered by the US Census. These rolling 1-year and 5-year estimates are meant to represent the characteristics of the population that change between each census.

The ACS asks participants a variety of demographic questions, such as their age, sex, race, household size, immigration status, and relationships to other occupants. However, the survey also includes detailed questions about a participant's employment, occupation, industry of work, income, health insurance status, and housing characteristics.

The ACS is a useful resource for determining aggregate measurements like an occupation's demographic profile, or average wages by region, education, and race.

For more information, see: https://www.census.gov/programs-surveys/acs.

American Time Use Survey. The American Time Use Survey is a survey commonly used to estimate the amount of time spent on household services for valuing losses in personal injury and wrongful death cases. The ATUS is sponsored by the US Bureau of Labor Statistics and administered by the Census Bureau. It measures the amount of time people spend doing various activities, such as paid work, childcare, volunteering, commuting, and socializing.

The survey was given to 21,000 individuals in 2003 and 14,000 individuals in 2004. It asks participants to account for every hour between 4 a.m. the day before the interview and 4 a.m. the day of the interview. Using this data, it is possible to construct the average hours spent on household services based on demographic characteristics. The categories most often used to measure household services are time spent:

- performing inside housework,
- cooking food and cleaning up after a meal,
- caring for pets, performing household maintenance, and maintaining vehicles
- managing the household
- shopping
- obtaining services
- traveling for household activities
- caring for and helping household children
- caring for and helping household adults
- caring for and helping non-household members
- traveling to care for and help household members, and
- traveling to care for and help non-household members.

For more information, see http://www.bls.gov/tus/home.htm.

Census. The Census is the largest survey in the United States. Conducted every ten years, the 2010 Census gathered information on 308.7 million people across the United States. The 100% characteristics form was asked of every person and housing unit in the United States. It includes information on sex, age, and race by geographic location. Census data is available at many different geographic levels including blocks, zip codes, county, and state.

More detailed questions are asked of a sample of persons and housing units. These questions include information on educational attainment, marital status, labor force status, and income. The Census is a very large database and hence has many uses, ranging from racial profiling, police stop baselines, to wage data.

For more information, see www.census.gov.

Census of Fatal Occupational Injuries. The Census of Fatal Occupational Injuries, provided by the Bureau of Labor Statistics, gives data on the number of fatal injuries on the job by the type of injury and by occupation, industry, or worker characteristics. This data is sometimes used to value a statistical life. Dangerous jobs tend to offer a wage premium in exchange for additional risk of death on the job. Some economists have attempted to quantify the value of life based on the additional wages that must be paid for a worker to accept an increased chance of a fatal accident.

For more information, see http://www.bls.gov/iif/oshcfoi1.htm.

Consumer Expenditure Survey. The Consumer Expenditure Survey is conducted for the US Census Bureau and the Bureau of Labor Statistics. It studies the expenditures, income, and household characteristics of American consumers. The CEX is often used in wrongful death cases to estimate a personal consumption factor.

The personal consumption factor is the amount of income the decedent would have spent on personal expenditures as opposed to income going to the household or other members of the household. Personal consumption includes expenditures on food, clothing, alcohol, transportation, etc. This factor is generally estimated using the expenditure data from CEX and regression analysis.

For more information, see http://www.bls.gov/cex.

Consumer Price Index. The Consumer Price Index is monthly data released by the Bureau of Labor Statistics on the change in prices paid by urban consumers for a representative basket of goods and services. The CPI is available by region and consumer type. It is most often used to measure inflation. Inflation becomes an important concern when present valuing economic damages in the future. Future damages must be discounted by the rate of inflation because $1 today is worth more than $1 tomorrow.

Note: even though CPIs differ by city, it is not appropriate to use CPI data to compare the cost of living between cities. The CPI does not measure price differentials between cities, only over time. The representative basket of goods and services varies based on geographic location.

For more information, see http://www.bls.gov/cpi.

Current Employment Statistics. The Current Employment Statistics program surveys roughly 160,000 businesses to provide detailed industry data on employment, hours, and earnings. This data is useful for determining the average amount of overtime worked by industry.

For more information, see http://www.bls.gov/ces.

Current Population Survey. The Current Population Survey is a monthly survey of roughly 50,000 households conducted by the Bureau of Labor Statistics and US Census Bureau. The CPS collects a vast amount of data and is an excellent resource for labor force characteristics.

The basic monthly survey of the CPS provides general demographic information as well as employment status, industry, and occupation. The monthly survey is often used to examine unemployment rates and the duration of unemployment. The BLS publishes tables that report the unemployment rate and average and median duration of unemployment by gender and age, race, or marital status. These tables are generally referenced in wrongful termination cases to show the length of time in which it is expected the Plaintiff will find a new job.

In addition to the basic monthly survey, the CPS also includes monthly supplements. These supplements include displaced workers, job tenure and mobility, and a demographic supplement (often referred to as the March supplement) just to name a few.

The job tenure supplement can be used to estimate the amount of time an individual would have likely remained at a job if the termination had not occurred. The demographic supplement is often used to determine average and median wages for particular education levels. Additionally, regression analysis can be used to estimate life cycle earnings for individuals based on their age or years of experience, education, and other pertinent demographic factors.

For more information, see http://www.bls.census.gov/cps.

Equal Employment Opportunity Census. The Equal Employment Opportunity Census is a tabulation created every ten years for the purpose of serving as an external benchmark for comparing the composition of a company's workforce to the external labor market within a specific geography and job category. The EEO Census provides worker counts based on race, ethnicity, gender, age, education level, industry, occupation, and geography. While the raw data is not readily available, 24 tables provide counts for varying cuts of the data.

The EEO Census is most often seen in Affirmative Action Plans and EEO Commission compliance reviews. It is also useful in the litigation setting to compare a defendant's workforce composition to the composition of comparable companies when there are discrimination allegations.

For more information, see: http://www.census.gov/hhes/www/eeo index/eeoindex.html.

Job Openings and Labor Turnover Survey. The Job Openings and Labor Turnover Survey is a monthly survey conducted by the Bureau of Labor Statistics. JOLTS collects data on total employment, the number of job openings, number of hires, and number of separations including quits and layoffs. JOLTS can be used to measure the growth of a particular industry and to get a better idea of labor market opportunities.

For more information, see http://www.bls.gov/jlt.

Local Area Unemployment Statistics. Local Area Unemployment Statistics available from the Bureau of Labor Statistics offers data on employment and unemployment for 7,200 geographic areas. Unemployment rates are available monthly by county, MSA, and state level. These rates may be compared over time to examine changes in the labor market.

Fore more information, see http://www.bls.gov/lau.

National Longitudinal Survey of Youth. The National Longitudinal Survey of Youth is a Bureau of Labor Statistics longitudinal study that repeatedly surveys approximately 12,000 individuals every two years. These individuals, who were selected at the beginning of the survey, are followed over time and surveyed on issues such as the individual's educational and employment experiences.

Ordered probit regressions and the NLSY can be used to estimate the probability of different levels of educational attainment. The probability of an individual obtaining a high school or college degree can be calculated based on demographic characteristics, such as race and gender, and household characteristics, such as family structure or parental educational attainment levels.

Regression analysis on NLSY data has also been used to estimate the length of time it takes for an individual's salary to catch up after an employment termination. This data can be used to determine the appropriate length of damages in wrongful termination cases.

For more information, see http://www.bls.gov/nls.

Occupational Employment Statistics. The Occupational Employment Statistics program conducted by the Bureau of Labor Statistics provides employment and wage information by occupation and geographic location. Hourly and annual mean and median wages are available for approximately 800 different occupations at the national, regional, state, and MSA level.

For more information, see http://www.bls.gov/oes.

Occupational Information Network. The Occupational Information Network is a government database of worker attributes and job characteristics. It is the replacement for the Dictionary of Occupational Titles. The database contains information about knowledge, skills, and ability requirements for various occupations as well as work environment conditions. The data can then be mapped to other occupational databases, such as the Equal Employment Opportunity Census and Occupational Employment Statistics, to determine how occupational skill requirements such as heavy lifting affect workforce composition, such as the gender distribution.

For more information, see http://www.onetcenter.org.

Panel Study of Income Dynamics. The Panel Study of Income Dynamics is a longitudinal survey conducted by the University of Michigan Institute for Social Research. The PSID has been following families since 1968 collecting data on economic, health, and social behavior. This data can be used for a multitude of purposes, including estimating the length of time for a worker's compensation to catch up following a termination.

For more information, see http://psidonline.isr.umich.edu.

Stock Based Employee Compensation

Abstract Stock based compensation is another component of pay for some individuals. In some cases, the terminated Plaintiff may have been in a job position that awarded employee stock options (ESOs) or stock grants. This chapter illustrates the application of various employee stock compensation models used to provide a valuation of the alleged breach of employment contract damages. In addition to ESO valuation, this chapter also illustrates the valuation of restricted company stock issues and provides a discussion of the approaches used to account for the unique valuation related issues that arise in litigation. A case example is used to demonstrate the methodologies used to value stock based compensation.

Keywords Intrinsic value · Black Scholes (B-S) · Lattice tree · Redemption behavior · Illiquidity discount

Stock based compensation is another component of pay for some individuals. In some cases, the terminated Plaintiff may have been in a job position that awarded employee stock options (ESOs) or stock grants. Other employees may have been enrolled in plans that made them eligible for participation in the employer's stock purchase plans. In this section, a case example is used to illustrate the methodologies used value stock based compensation.

Specifically, in this chapter, we consider a case study for a former CEO of a large telecommunication company who filed a lawsuit against her former employer. In her lawsuit she alleged that the company's contract breach resulted in the loss of ESO grants and diminished the value of the vested ESOs that she held at the time of the alleged contract breach. The former company executive also alleges that the breach prevented her from receiving restricted company stock shares that she believes she was entitled to under her contract with the employer.

This chapter illustrates the application of various employee stock compensation models used to provide a valuation of the alleged breach of employment contract damages. In addition to ESO valuation, this paper also illustrates the valuation of restricted company stock issues and provides a discussion of the approaches used to account for the unique valuation related issues that arise in litigation. The case study illustrates the importance of incorporating case specific factors, such as the Plaintiff's historical ESO exercise rates and firm specific ESO forfeiture probabilities, into the valuation models.

INTRODUCTION

In contrast to a typical employee, the compensation package for CEOs, CFOs, and other company executives is routinely composed of stock based incentives such as employee stock options (ESO)and stock grants. Research on CEO compensation packages has shown that stock comprised over 60% of executives at a 'new economy' firms such as computer and telecommunication firms, and over 40% in 'old economy' firms such as manufacturing and energy companies. The goal of this paper is to provide a case study that demonstrates the use of two frequently utilized employee stock option valuation methods to evaluate economic damages in a litigation setting.

Specifically, this case study involves a breach of employment contract lawsuit that was filed by the former CEO of a large telecommunication company. In the lawsuit, the CEO alleges that the telecommunication company's breach of employment contract resulted in the loss of ESO grants and diminished the value of the vested ESOs that the CEO held at the time of the alleged contract breach. The former company executive also alleges that the breach prevented her from receiving restricted company stock shares that she believes she was entitled to under her contract with the employer. In this case study, the economic damage methodologies utilized by the Plaintiff and defense experts in the employment contract breach lawsuit are compared and contrasted.

In the first section of the case study, the background on the parties and allegations in the lawsuit is discussed. In the second and third sections of this case study, the Plaintiff and defense experts' economic damages models related to the Plaintiffs unexercised and exercised employee stock option grants are presented. In the fourth section, both parties' economic expert's valuations of the economic damages related to the Plaintiff's restriction stock incentives are compared and contrasted.

Case Study Background

This case study involves a breach of employment contract lawsuit that was filed by the retired, former CEO of a large telecommunication company. The Plaintiff's employment contract stated that she would receive an annual salary, bonuses, and stock based compensation. According to the Plaintiff, the company reneged on its contractual obligation to award her 335,000 employee stock options and 125,000 shares of restricted stock. In contrast to a typical employee grant, the ESO grants at issue would have been immediately vested, or exercisable, and had a five year exercise period. Stock options cannot generally be exercised until they are vested. Typically, ESOs have a three to ten year expiration period and vest over a period of years. For instance, a ESO grant may state that a certain percentage per year of the options will vest per year.

The defendant argues that the company, under the Plaintiff's term as CEO, did not meet certain financial performance goals that were required for the issuance of the ESOs or restricted shares of stock. The undisputed facts in the case show that while the Plaintiff was the CEO, the company underwent extensive Internal Revenue Service and Security Exchange Commission financial audits. Following the audits, the company was required to restate its earnings for the previous five-year reporting period. The company argues that it was required by law to impose an ESO issue and redemption 'black-out' period during the restatement period. During the black-out period, which lasted 18 months, the company did not redeem any outstanding employee stock options, issue any new employee stock options, or issue any new stock.

Table 1 Employee stock compensation at issue in breach of contract lawsuit

Stock based employee compensation	Quantity
Unawarded employee stock options	335,000
Vested employee stock options	873,916
Unvested employee stock options	95,375
Restricted stock	125,000

The CEO also alleges that the ESO redemption black-out period imposed by the defendant lowered the value of the vested and unvested employee stock options that she held. The CEO's records show that on the day that the black-out period was imposed, she had three years to exercise 873,916 vested employee stock options. In addition, she also had 95,375 unvested employee stock options that were due to vest in six months. Once vested, she had five years to exercise the ESOs. The CEO ultimately exercised all of her outstanding employee stock options after the blackout period was lifted. However, she argues that had she been able to redeem her ESOs earlier she would have realized greater returns.

Table 1 shows the number of allegedly unawarded ESOs, vested ESOs, and the restricted stock that the CEO believes that she should have received.

Analysis of Plaintiff's Allegations

Breach of Contract Allegation 1: Failure to award 335,000 ESOs

To assess the economic damages associated with this allegation, both the defendant's and the Plaintiff's economic experts developed economic valuations of the ESOs that the Plaintiff alleges that she should have been awarded. The Plaintiff's expert economic valuation was based on an analysis of the intrinsic value of the ESO as of the date he performed his valuation. The defendant's analysis was based on the option pricing value of the employee stock options as of the date of the alleged breach. The expert's methodologies, results, and discussion in presented in the following sections.

Plaintiff's Expert Analysis
The Plaintiff's expert intrinsic value analysis was based on an assumed ESO grant price (strike price) and an assumed company stock sell price

(spot price). The Plaintiff's expert opined that the company's failure to award the CEO 335,000 ESOs resulted in an economic loss of $4,582,800 to the Plaintiff.

In his analysis, the Plaintiff's expert assumed that had the CEO received the ESOs, the ESOs would have had a grant price, or the amount that the employee pays to purchase the shares of stock from the company, that was equal to the closing price on the day that the ESOs would have been issued. The company's stock shares were trading at $7.55 per share on the day that the CEO alleges that she would have received the ESO grants. The Plaintiff's expert based his assume sell price on the company's stock price ($21.23 per share) on the date in which he produced his economic damage report.

Defendant Expert Analysis
The defense expert utilized three commonly used employee stock option pricing models to provide a valuation of the alleged damages. The defendant's economic expert used the standard Black Scholes (B-S), the modified B-S Shapiro and O'Connor model, and the Hull and White binomial ESO valuation model to provide three separate estimates. In each of the analyses, the defense expert also calculated the value of the ESOs as of the date that the CEO would have allegedly received the ESOs. The defendant's expert's analysis is found in Table 2 in a later section of this paper.

The option pricing models used to estimate the CEOs alleged damages are described below.

Black Scholes (B-S) ESO valuation models
One model that was used in this case is referred to as the Black Scholes (B-S) ESO valuation model. The value of an employee stock option can be approximated using the standard B-S call option (C) formula. In general, the B-S ESO model is based on a number of factors. These factors include the current stock price, an interest rate factor, the time until expiration of the option in years, the stock option exercise price, and volatility of the employer/defendant's underlying stock price. In addition these factors, the ESO specific vesting period will also impact the value of the ESO.

Lattice Tree ESO Valuation Models
In addition to the standard B-S and the B-S model with vesting, a lattice tree pricing model was also used to estimate the value of the allegedly

unawarded ESOs. Lattice tree models use estimates of stock price movements over time to estimate year end share prices and ultimately ESO values. In these models, the stock price movements are based on the expected volatility of the company's stock price.

ESO values in lattice tree models are determined by first calculating the share price at the end of each year in the lattice tree. The ESO value at each year, or node of the tree, is determined by calculating the expected return at each node of the tree. The expected value is determined using the probability of upward and downward stock price movements and the risk-free interest rate. The final value of the ESO is determined by moving backwards in the lattice tree.

Generally, the value of an ESO calculated from the lattice will be impacted by the company's stock price volatility, the employee's exercise behavior, vesting period, ESO forfeiture rates, and interest rates. All other factors equal, higher company stock price volatility increases the value of an ESO because higher volatility creates a greater probability of upward stock price movements. The value of an ESO decreases as the employee's option exercise multiple (stock price/exercise price) decreases because the individuals require a relatively lower rate of return before the ESO is exercised by the employee. Longer vesting periods which increase the expected exercise time ultimately increases the value of ESOs. Higher ESO forfeiture rates, such as those due to employee attrition, decrease the value of ESOs. Interest rates are inversely related to ESO values due to the time value of money.

Table 2 presents the ESO values for each of the models estimated by the Plaintiff and defense experts. As the table shows, the intrinsic valuation approach yielded the highest valuation and the binomial approach yielded the smallest estimate of the value of the CEOS's unawarded ESOs. As is consistent with the literature, the B-S model generated values that were higher than the binomial model. The unadjusted B-S and the binomial model valuation differential was approximately 18.6% while the vesting adjusted ESO model resulted in valuations that were lower than the unadjusted B-S model but higher than the binomial model.

Table 2 Analysis of damages related to unawarded ESOs

Model	ESO Value	Total economic damage (335,000 ESOs)
Defense ESO valuation models		
Black Scholes (B-S)	$2.31	$773,852
Shapiro and Reid (2001) B-S	$2.13	$713,721
Hull and White (2004) lattice tree	$1.88	$629,803
Plaintiff's ESO valuation model		
Intrinsic value ($21.23–$7.55)	$13.68	$4,582,800

Breach of Contract Allegation 2: Company damaged the value of outstanding ESOs

In addition to the unawarded ESO allegation, the CEO also complained about the damaged value of the ESOs that she held at the time of the 18 month stock trading black out. As mentioned, the company was not allowed to redeem any employee stock options during this time period. The CEO alleges that had she been able to exercise her options during this black-out period she would have realized a higher gain than she actually did from her options.

As shown in Table 1, at the time that the black-out period was instituted the CEO held a total of 969,291 vested and unvested ESOs. Both the vested and unvested ESOs had a grant price of $11.23 and had three years remaining on the exercise period. The unvested ESOs vested 6 months after the black-out period was instituted.

Plaintiffs Expert Analysis
The Plaintiff's expert used an intrinsic value approach to value the alleged damage done to the CEO's outstanding ESOs. In the analysis, the Plaintiff's expert bases his analysis on the company's stock price on the date that the Plaintiff alleges that she wanted to exercise her stock options. He opines that the CEO has incurred economic damages of $5,414,073 to the value of her outstanding ESO grants.

The CEO testified that on a particular day, which was during the 18 month black-out period, she contacted her broker and inquired if the black-out period concerning the redemption of ESO grants was still in place. She stated that on this date she wanted to exercise her employee options (all the options were exercisable at this date) but was denied by the company. On this date the company's stock was traded at $21.56 per share.

Over a several month period, the CEO was able to exercise her options after the black-out period ended. Accordingly, the Plaintiff's expert estimated the alleged damage to the CEO's ESO value as the difference between the amount that she would have realized had she sold during the blackout period, $10,012,776, and the amount that she actually realized from the sale of her ESOs, $4,598,703.

Defendant Expert Analysis

The defense expert utilized the option pricing models described above to assess the value of the alleged damage to the CEO's outstanding ESOs. The defense expert based his calculation on the difference between the value of the ESOs at the beginning of the black-out period and the value of the ESOs at the end of the black-out period. The analysis is shown in Table 3.

As the table shows, the defense expert opined that the CEO incurred no damage to her outstanding ESO grants, vested and unvested. This is because the analysis showed that the ESOs, which were under water, i.e. had no monetary value, at the beginning of the black-out period, actually

Table 3 Defense expert's analysis of damage to outstanding vested ESOs using Hull-White model

Model	ESO value	Number of vested options	Value of vested options
Time period			
Before company imposed stock trading black-out period	$1.28	873,916	$1,041,812
After company imposed stock trading black-out period	$3.45	873,916	$2,808,010
		Economic Damage	−$1,766,198

The Hull and White (2004) lattice tree model uses the same parameters as the B-S model described in Table 2 in addition to $M = 1.5$ and $(q\delta t) = .0777$

increased in value after the black-out period. In this example, the Plaintiff and defense expert's analyses are very clearly different.

The specific valuations were derived as follows. On the day prior to the imposition of the black-out period, company's stock was trading at $9.34 which was lower than the grant price ($11.23) of the CEO's outstanding ESOs. Based on these stock prices, the parameters discussed in the previous section, and a three year expiration period, the lattice tree model yields a value of $1.28 for the CEO's outstanding ESOs prior to the imposition of the black-out period. After the 18 month black-out period, the company's stock price increased to $13.76. Based on these stock prices, the parameters discussed in the previous section, and a 18 month expiration period, the lattice tree model values the CEO's outstanding ESOs at $3.48 at the end of the black-out period. The Black–Scholes based ESO pricing models produced similar results. The valuation of the alleged damage to the unvested options was performed in a similar manner.

Discussion
Clearly the substantial difference in the economic damages opinions provided by the Plaintiffs and defense experts are driven by the significant differences in the methods that were employed. The Plaintiff's intrinsic value approach is appealing because it provides a concrete estimate of the return that the CEO under one scenario would have actually realized had they been awarded the ESOs. However, the approach suffers from the fact that there is no objective reason to believe that the CEO would have actually exercised the stock option on the day that the expert selected. The Plaintiff's approach implicitly assumes that the CEO would have had perfect foresight to be able to realize the gains suggested by the intrinsic model. It is possible that the CEO would have selected another date to exercise the stock options that would conceivable lead to a smaller rate of return and lower damages.

The defendant's expert's option pricing approach is appealing because it takes into account the possibility that the CEO could have exercised the stock options at any point within the exercise period. Further, since the valuation is done as of the date that the options would have been awarded, the option pricing approach is more consistent with the underlying damage concept of making the individual whole as of the date of the breach of contract. The defendant's approach suffers from the fact that the damages derived from the ESO model are conceptual and not actual hard dollars that were lost by the Plaintiff. Since the ESOs are not actually tradable or transferrable, the Plaintiff could not have actually sold the options to realize the returns suggested by the option pricing model.

Furthermore in this case, the estimate of the expected volatility of the company stock was of concern in the valuation of the ESOs using the option pricing models. Generally volatility is measured using either historical stock price data or is implied from the market prices of the company's options the observed in the market. Under the implied volatility approach, the Black Scholes option pricing model is used in reverse to calculate the market's opinion of the company's stock's underlying volatility. In this case, the company did not have any public stock options to observe, so the historical data approach was used.

In a litigation setting, the past employee stock option redemption behavior can be particularly useful. In particular the CEO's past ESO exercise patterns were used to estimate the actual stock price to grant price multiples in which the CEO exercised previous ESO grants. On average, the CEO's previous ESOs were exercised when the stock was 1.5 times the grant price. Past ESO redemption behavior can also be used to assess the reasonableness of assumptions used in intrinsic valuations of ESOs.

The prominent position of the Plaintiff within the company and the large number of stock involved, suggested that several other conceptual ESO valuation issues be addressed. First, the CEO was a key executive in the company and exerted managerial control over the company. In this types of situations, research suggest that an investigation into the possible relationship between the extent of the CEO's control over the company and company stock price should be undertaken.

Second, some research suggests that the ESO forfeiture rate may change after the vesting occurs. For instance, before the option is vested the employee may be more likely to leave the company or other forfeit the option since the ESOs were not exercisable. Conversely, an employee may be less likely to forfeit an option after vesting since they potentially may be foregoing financial gains. However, additional information on the actual ESO forfeiture and employee tenure would be needed to determine if this factor is indeed an issue.

Third, there may be a correlation between the probability of an employee exiting the company, the resulting forfeiture rate, and the company's profitability that needs to be accounted for in the analysis. Huddart and Lang (1996) suggest that employees in more profitable companies may be less likely to leave and forego the perceived greater likelihood of increased profitability in the future.

Fourth, in cases such as this, where there are a large number of ESOs at issue, issues related to stock dilution need to be considered in the analysis. In this case, the amount of allegedly unawarded ESOs was relatively large when compared to the daily trading volume of the company's stock. In fact, the Plaintiff's stock broker testified he would not be able to sell all of the CEO's shares on one date without depressing the company's stock price.

Breach of Contract Allegation 3: Failure to award restricted stock

Finally, the executive alleges that she should have received 125,000 shares of restricted stock from the company. The restricted stock at issue required that the CEO hold the stock for one year before it could be sold.

Plaintiff Expert's Analysis
The Plaintiff's expert examined the value of the restricted stock on the date it would have been issued to the CEO. Based on the $11.45 share price, the 125,000 restricted shares were valued at $1,431,250 by the Plaintiff's expert.

Defense Expert's Analysis
The defense expert examined the value of the restricted stock as of the date of issue but also accounted for the illiquidity discount factor associated with the one year trading restriction. That is, assuming that the CEO would have received the shares she would not have been able to immediately sell the stock on the date of issue. Based on an illiquidity discount factor that ranged between 0.75 and 0.90, The defense expert estimated that the value of the CEO's restricted stock was between $1,073,438 and $1,288,125.

Discussion
Generally, illiquidity discount factors are calculated using stock options and/or guidelines from IRS tax cases. Stock option based approaches use the discount implied from a futures option on the company's stock to determine illiquidity discounts. If the company actually has publicly traded futures options then the market values of the options can be used

to determine the amount of the discount. Illiquidity discount factors between 10 and 40% have been found to be acceptable in IRS tax cases.

In this case, the company did not have publically traded options so no market based discount could be calculated. For simplicity purposes, the low end illiquidity discount factor range suggested by the literature was selected and used in the analysis.

Conclusions

This case study has shown the application of the Shapiro and O'Connor modified Black–Scholes (B-S) and the Hull-White binomial lattice tree employee stock option (ESO) valuation models to the valuation of economic damages in an employment breach of contract case. Approaches used to account for the unique ESO valuation related issues that arise in litigation were discussed. The case study illustrated the importance of incorporating case specific factors, such as the Plaintiff's historical ESO exercise rates and firm specific ESO forfeiture probabilities, into the valuation models.

The following articles and research papers provide additional insights and information concerning the valuation of employee stock options.

Employee Stock Options References

Aboody, David. "Market Valuation of Employee Stock Options." *Journal of Accounting & Economics* 22 (1996): 357–391.

Barenbaum, Les, Walt Schubert, and Bonnie O'Rourke. "Valuing Employee Stock Options Using a Lattice Model." *The CPA Journal* December (2004): n. pag. *New York State Society of CPAa*. Web. 10 Dec. 2009.

Brous, Peter. "Estimating Damages Associated with Stock Option Compensation in Wrongful Termination Lawsuits." *Journal of Forensic Economics* 15.3 (2002): 269–283.

Carpenter, Jennifer. "The Exercise and Valuation of Executive Stock Options." *Journal of Financial Economics* 48 (1998): 127–158.

Consulting, Radford. "FAS 123 (R) Disclosures - 997% Increase in the Use of Binomial Models Since 2003." *Radford Consulting* 1 (2008): n. pag. *Radford*. Web. 11 Dec. 2008.

Cuny, C., and P. Jarion. "Valuing Executive Stock Options with An Endogenous Departure Decision." *Journal of Accounting and Economics* 20 (1995): 127–158.

Cvitanic, Jasksa, Zvi Wiener, and Fernando Zapatero. "Analytic Pricing of Employee Stock Options." *Review of Financial Studies* 21.2 (2008): 683–724.

Damodaran, Aswath. "Employee Stock Options (ESOPS) and Restricted Stock Effects and Consequences", *Stern School of Business Working Paper* (2005).

Damodaran, Aswath. "Marketability and Value: Measuring the Illiquidity Discount", *Stern School of Business Working Paper* (2005).

Finnerty, John. "Extending the Black-Scholes-Merton Model to Value Employee Stock Options." *Journal of Applied Finance* 15.2 (2005): 1–20.

Hall, Brian, and Kevin Murphy. "The Trouble with Stock Options." *Journal of Economic Perspectives* 17.3 (2003): 49–70.

Huddart, Steven, and Mike Lang. "Employee Stock Option Exercises: An Empirical Analysis." *Journal of Accounting and Economics* 21 (1996): 5–43.

Huddart, Steven. "Employee Stock Options." *Journal of Accounting & Economics* 18 (1994): 207–231.

Hull, John, and Alan White. "How to Value Employee Stock Options." *Financial Analysts Journal*, 60.1 (2004): 114–119.

Hull, John. *Options, Futures and Other Derivatives*, 5th ed. Boston, MA: Prentice Hall College Div, 2002.

Johnson, George, and David Dufendach. "Valuation of Options on Restricted Stock Using Simple Modifications of the Black-Scholes Model." *Business Valuation Review*, 17.2 (1998): 35–41.

Lambert, Richard, David Larcker, and Robert Verrecchia. "Portfolio Considerations in Valuing Executive Compensation." *Journal of Accounting Research*, 29.1 (1991): 129–149

Mun, Johnathan. *Valuing Employee Stock Options (Wiley Finance)*. New York, NY: Wiley, 2004.

Reid, Sean, Matthew O'Connor, and Steven Shapiro. "The Valuation of Employee Stock Options Issued by Closely Held Firms." *Journal of Legal Economics* April (2006): 1–5.

Shapiro, Steven, and Matthew O'Connor. "Employee Stock Options as a Source of Compensation." *Litigation Economics Review*, 5.1 (2001): 11–18.

Williams, David. "Valuing the Components of the Compensation Package of Executives." *Litigation Economics Review*, 3.2 (1998): 85–99.

Analysis Information Requirements

Abstract In order to estimate the Plaintiff's lost earnings in an employment termination case, there are a number of essential components that must be addressed. These components are the total compensation that the employee would have been expected to receive had their employment not been terminated, the employee's attempts to find replacement employment, the total compensation they can be expected to earn now in their replacement employment, and the determined present value of the potential future losses. This section includes a list of commonly required documents, guidelines on collecting information, a sample employment termination case information checklist, and sample plaintiff interrogatory questions.

Keywords Information collection · Required documents · Guidelines · Checklist · Sample questions

In order to estimate the Plaintiff's lost earnings in an employment termination case, there are a number of essential components that must be addressed. These components are the total compensation that the employee would have been expected to receive had their employment not been terminated, the employee's attempts to find replacement employment, the total compensation they can be expected to earn now in their replacement employment, and the determined present value of the potential future losses. Listed below are the documents which are most commonly required in order to address the first two components of a Plaintiff's alleged back and front pay losses.

Information Typically Needed

- Individual tax returns, such as 1040, 1040A, 3 to 5 years if available
- Business tax returns, such as 1120 and 1040—Schedule C, 3 to 5 years if available
- Employer-provided pay statements, for previous and current employment
- IRS, W-2 wage, and 1099-Misc income statements, 3 to 5 years if available
- 401 k balance statements, following employment termination and most recent
- Retirement plan summary plan description(s)
- Employee stock option grant letters
- Stock option exercise letters
- Employee handbooks
- Social Security Administration SA earnings statements, most recent
- Job description (includes description of duties, responsibilities and relevant employer organization)
- Job ladders for relevant portion of employer
- Company, especially human resources, representatives depositions
- Job search logs to document post-termination job search
- Emails regarding job search and job applications

Guidelines on Collecting Information for Lost Earnings Analyses in Employment Termination Cases

Documents should be collected directly from the government agency and employer when possible. Not all employees maintain a full set of pay stubs or financial records for the required number of years.

Use multiple data sources to corroborate the financial picture. For example, use the 1040 tax return statement in conjunction with the W-2 wage and income statements. Looking at multiple sets of information allows for the separation of the income of multiple filers. Comparing the entries on both sets of documents will also enable the isolation and removal of income that is inappropriately reducing or increasing the subject's projected earnings.

Valuation of retirement accounts will generally require a detailed employee benefits handbook. Obtain the summary plan description for the retirement plan.

If possible, the cost of providing benefits should be directly obtained from the employer. The actual benefits data can provide an alternative to the standard salary multiplier measure, which is based on the average employer cost of providing benefits.

To obtain an accurate projection of but-for employment termination earnings, it is important to obtain information from the years that best describe the subject's earnings potential during the time at issue. For some cases, this may be three years of historical data, but in other instances it may be the last three months of salary data if for example the subject just began a new job.

Sample Employment Termination Case Information Checklist

Complete for job position at time of termination and each employer since employment termination

Company name						
Hire date	Month	Day		Year		
Wage/salary at hire			Hourly		Weekly	Annually
Job title at hire						
Typical job duties at hire						
Termination date	Month	Day		Year		
Wage / salary at termination			Hourly		Weekly	Annually
Job title at termination						

(continued)

(continued)

Typical job duties at termination			
Union job?	Yes	No	
Hours worked per week			
Average tips per hour			
Health benefits	Yes	No	Unknown
Dental benefits	Yes	No	Unknown
Vision benefits	Yes	No	Unknown
Life benefits	Yes	No	Unknown
Defined contribution plans (401 k plans)	Yes	No	Unknown
Defined benefit plans (pension plans)	Yes	No	Unknown
Employee stock options	Yes	No	Unknown
Employee stock purchase	Yes	No	Unknown

Sample Plaintiff Interrogatory Questions

Defendants in employment termination cases will in many cases need to obtain post-employment information from the Plaintiff during discovery by using interrogatory questions and the related production that the Plaintiffs provided.

Below are examples of interrogatory questions that can be used to assist in the production of the documents needed for an economic analysis of the Plaintiff's potential back and front pay losses.

- Please identify all businesses, ventures, and entrepreneurial activities not related to the Defendant that you have engaged in and received compensation in connection with while working for the Defendant.
- Provide documentation concerning: (i) communications with potential employers; (ii) job search efforts; and (iii) offers of employment, including offered income and benefits.

- Describe your efforts to secure employment from the time of your termination to the present, identifying the places to which you applied for employment, interviews received, the persons with whom you interviewed, and any offers of employment you received.
- Please identify each employer (including self-employment) for whom you worked since last employed by the Defendant, including the beginning and ending dates of employment and reason(s) for any termination of employment.
- For each employer identified above, please state the job duties, wages, and responsibilities you had at each employer.
- State every source of income (including, but not limited to wages, commissions, unemployment benefits, investments, and any other compensation) since your termination from the defendant, state the basis for the payment received, dates received, amounts received, and the identity of any employer. Describe any supporting document.

Case Study 1: Registered Nurse v. Health Science Center

Abstract This case study provides an example where the Plaintiff would be expected to incur little to no future economic losses due to the abundance of replacement employment opportunities available at the time of separation. The Plaintiff in this case was a Registered Nurse (RN), which is a highly skilled position that requires years of medical training and certification. Because of the job requirements of a RN, it was important to look at the job market specific to Plaintiff's education and training. The labor market availability study performed in this case found that had the Plaintiff performed a sufficiently diligent job search, she could have been expected to find comparable replacement employment within a reasonable period of time.

Keywords Inadequate job search · Registered nurse (RN) · Highly skilled employee · Health industry · Transferable skills · Unemployment insurance

In Brief

This case study provides an example where the Plaintiff would be expected to incur little to no future economic losses due to the abundance of

© The Author(s), under exclusive license to Springer Nature Switzerland AG 2022
D. Steward, *Economic Losses and Mitigation after an Employment Termination*,
https://doi.org/10.1007/978-3-030-88364-5_9

replacement employment opportunities available at the time of separation. The Plaintiff in this case was a Registered Nurse (RN), which is a highly skilled position that requires years of medical training and certification. Because of the job requirements of a RN, it was important to look at the job market specific to Plaintiff's education and training. The labor market availability study performed in this case found that had the Plaintiff performed a sufficiently diligent job search, she could have been expected to find comparable replacement employment within a reasonable period of time.

Background

The Plaintiff in this case, Ms. Phoebe Roberts, was employed as a Clinical Instructor at an academic health science center. The Plaintiff provided W2 tax statements which showed she made $58,271 in total compensation in her last full year of employment. As a Clinical Instructor, Ms. Robert's job duties included classroom teaching, and observing and instructing medical treatment by paramedics.

In this position, Ms. Roberts was also certified as an Registered Nurse and as an Emergency Trauma RN. At the time of her separation, Ms. Roberts had over 15 years of experience as an RN, of which over 10 years were as an Emergency Trauma RN. Ms. Roberts's resume showed that she had been employed with recognized major medical employers throughout her career as an RN. In her deposition, the Plaintiff provided important details on her job functions and duties while employed at the defendant employer.

Q: It sounds to me like one of the things that you were required to do would be to teach classes, right? Would that be in a classroom setting?
A: Yes, sir. In a classroom setting.
Q: Okay. And I'm not going to hold you to hard and fast numbers. But if you can give me a sense of the rough percentage of your job that involved teaching in a classroom, and about how much of your time was spent in the field?
A: About 12 hours of teaching time in the classroom. And then approximately, averaging it out, I was riding out in the field about 20 hours a week on top of that.
Q: Okay. But you were a full-time employee?

A: Yes, technically 40 hours was supposed to be what we were and then obviously if things in a salary position came up, you know, late meetings. There were some other things on top of that I spent some time on.

The Plaintiff's qualifications as both an RN and a Clinical Instructor provides her with employment opportunities not only in a medical setting but also an educational setting as well. Since her separation from the defendant employer, the Plaintiff was unemployed for 14 months before she began working as an RN at a medical center, as well as working at her father's contracting company.

Analysis

Using employment statistics and labor markets, it was shown that the Plaintiff had not performed an adequate search for replacement employment. While unemployed, Ms. Roberts applied for relatively few job positions and relatively few employers following her separation from the defendant employer. The table below shows all of the positions that Ms. Roberts reported applying for during her 14 month period of unemployment. As shown in the table, in at least two months during this period, Ms. Roberts reported that she did not apply for a single job position.

Ms. Roberts's Job Search, June 1, 2011 to August 1, 2012

Date applied	Job position (if listed)
09/10/2011	ER RN, house supervisor
10/07/2011	Education specialist
12/15/2011	Team manager, cardiac division
01/16/2012	Sent application
02/02/2012	ER RN
02/10/2012	Sent application
03/06/2012	Sent application
03/24/2012	RN health nurse
03/30/2012	Instructor
04/03/2012	Regulatory RN
06/06/2012	Nurse analyst
06/12/2012	Sent application

Further, documents from the state workforce agency indicated that Ms. Roberts was not eligible for unemployment benefits in four of the weeks in which she applied for benefits. In those weeks, Ms. Roberts did not perform the required job search activity and was not eligible for benefits under the state's unemployment rules. In the weeks where she did receive benefits, Ms. Roberts stated that she searched for the minimum number of job searches required to receive unemployment benefits. When asked about her job search in her deposition, Ms. Roberts testified the following:

Q: Did you get unemployment?
A: Yes, I did.
Q: For how long?
A: In total, it was ten months.
Q: Did the [State Workforce Agency] require you to perform a minimum number of work search activities in order to receive unemployment benefits?
A: Yes. I had to look for three jobs per week.
Q: How many job search activities did you typically do per week?
A: Three. I met the requirements.

Although the Plaintiff's job search does not reflect it, there were employers of various sizes in her geographical area which had openings for RNs at the time of her separation from the defendant employer. In the metropolitan statistical area (MSA) in which Ms. Roberts lived, TWC and BLS data tabulations indicate that there were at least 201 RN job openings in a typical month in the year she was terminated. The typical wages associated with these RN job positions is comparable to, if not greater than, the compensation that Ms. Roberts earned at the defendant employer at the time of her separation.

Tabulations using microdata, or data tracking statistics to specific individuals, from the BLS Current Population Survey was used to calculate the wages that individuals similarly situated to Ms. Roberts reported earning. At the time that Ms. Roberts was terminated, Register Nurses with similar experience and in her MSA reported that they earned on average $64,000. Other sources, such as Salary.com, indicates that RNs in her geographical area typically received total compensation in the range of $58,291 to $63,470.

Labor market research and studies further demonstrate the high employer demand for RNs that existed at the time Ms. Roberts's employment was terminated. For instance, an independent agency conducted a Hospital Nurse Staffing Survey and found that her labor market region had an RN vacancy rate of 12.6%, and a 20.9% increase in the overall position vacancy rate for RNs during Ms. Roberts's period of unemployment. Other labor market studies, such as those performed by Wanted Analytics, reported that hiring demand for RNs was up by more than 56% in the year that Ms. Roberts was terminated.

In this case, Ms. Roberts's reported period of unemployment and/or underemployment is inconsistent with the strong employer demand that exists for her knowledge, skills, abilities, and experience. The typical RN in Ms. Roberts's MSA could have been expected to find replacement employment within 6 weeks of starting a sufficient job search. Overall, BLS data shows employees in her MSA typically can expect to find replacement employment within 15 weeks.

In conclusion, had Ms. Roberts performed a sufficiently diligent job search, she could have been expected to find replacement employment in a reasonable amount of time, and would have incurred little to no future economic losses.

Case Study 2: Truck Driver v. Concrete Mixing Company

Abstract In this case, the Plaintiff, Mr. Marvin Franklin, worked as a Truck Driver with a concrete mixing company. Mr. Franklin alleges that his employment was terminated by the employer due to his age. Mr. Franklin was unemployed for two years following his employment termination. Mr. Franklin subsequently obtained replacement employment as a factory worker and earned approximately half as much as he did driving trucks for the Defendant.

Keywords Expected unemployment duration · State workforce data · Trucking industry · Labor market boundaries · Job search effort

In Brief

In this case, the Plaintiff, Mr. Marvin Franklin, worked as a Truck Driver with a concrete mixing company. Mr. Franklin alleges that his employment was terminated by the employer due to his age. Mr. Franklin was unemployed for two years following his employment termination. Mr. Franklin subsequently obtained replacement employment as a factory worker and earned approximately half as much as he did driving trucks for the Defendant.

An analysis of Mr. Franklin's job search efforts and employment was performed in this case. Our analysis revealed that there were a number of available jobs that Mr. Franklin could have applied for and been qualified to hold. Mr. Franklin's deposition testimony and job search records indicate that he was not diligent or consistent in his job search following the cessation of his employment with the Defendant. Furthermore, the labor market for Mr. Franklin's expertise indicated that he was substantially underemployed and could have been expected to obtain a job position with higher salary had he performed a sufficiently diligent job search.

Background

In this case, the Plaintiff Mr. Marvin Franklin worked as a Truck Driver with a concrete mixing company. Mr. Franklin alleges that his employment was terminated by the employer due to his age. Mr. Franklin was 53 at the time his employment ended with the Defendant. As a Truck Driver, Mr. Franklin's job duties included driving cement trucks and dump trucks to and from various locations. Mr. Franklin was an hourly worker and received an hourly wage of $22.50 at the time his employment ended. Mr. Franklin's previous employment included several factory jobs after he graduated high school. Mr. Franklin had previously worked as a Forklift Operator and as a Laborer prior to his employment as a Truck Driver. Mr. Franklin did attend truck driving courses at a community college and obtained a Class B Commercial Driving License (CDL).

After his employment as a Truck Driver ended, Mr. Franklin was unemployed for nearly four years until he found employment as a Factory Worker. As a Factory Worker, Mr. Franklin was not required to perform any driving duties and did not require Mr. Franklin to hold a Class B CDL. Mr. Franklin, as a Factory Worker, receives $10.40 per hour, less than half of what he earned as a Truck Driver. Mr. Franklin did not provide job search records in this matter. Deposition testimony was used to determine the extent of the job search performed by Mr. Franklin.

Analysis

The first step in the analysis is to determine the relevant labor market that was available to Mr. Franklin. Mr. Franklin lived in a rural area of Illinois that was about 150 miles south of Chicago. Mr. Franklin held a CDL and had been working as a Truck Driver for over eight years at the time of his job search.

Information from the Illinois Department of Employment Security provided data on the number of typical job openings each year for job positions that Mr. Franklin would have been qualified to hold. In addition, The Bureau of Labor Statistics Occupational Outlook Handbook identified several occupations similar to that of Truck Driver that Mr. Franklin would have been qualified to hold. Those occupations included Heavy and Tractor-Trailer Truck Drivers, Bus Drivers, Delivery Truck Drivers and Driver/Sales Workers, Hand Laborers and Material Movers, Railroad Workers, and Water Transportation Workers. Our research found that in the Local Workforce Investment Area (LWIA) in which Mr. Franklin lived, there were more than 14 job openings per month for these related occupations and more than eight job openings per month for Truck Drivers.

Numerous job openings also existed for these job positions in the areas surrounding Mr. Franklin's direct city of residence. Research found that in the LWIA surrounding Mr. Franklin's resident city, there were many additional job openings that Mr. Franklin would have been able to apply to. In the surrounding LWIA's, there were more than 32 job openings per month for Bus Drivers, Delivery Truck Drivers and Driver/Sales Workers, Hand Laborers and Material Movers, Railroad Workers, and Water Transportation Workers. The surrounding LWIA's near where Mr. Franklin lived had approximately 16 job openings per month for Truck Drivers.

Data indicated that these Truck Driver positions have average wages of $26.54 per hour. The additional job positions identified as similar to Truck Driver positions have average wages between $14.67 and $24.25. These earnings were similar to the earnings that Mr. Franklin had during his employment with the defendant.

Additionally, there were also many employers in the Concrete, Trucking, and Distribution industry similar to the concrete mixing company that Mr. Franklin had previously been employed with. A Google maps search was performed in this matter to determine the companies Mr. Franklin could have sought employment through. The Google search indicated that there were 43 employers that were in the Concrete, Trucking, and Distribution industry in the area where Mr. Franklin lived.

Mr. Franklin did not attempt to seek employment from even a portion of these employers. Mr. Franklin had an extremely limited view of the employers that he could have sought employment, as illustrated in the deposition excerpt below.

> **Q:** So, what did you do to find another driving job?
> **A:** I didn't get another driving job.
> **Q:** Why not?
> **A:** I would have had to move out of this area. I mean, it's either [DEFENDANT] or the county.
> **Q:** That's the only two people who can put you to work with a Class B CDL?
> **A:** In the concrete field in a mixer, that's what I would had to have did. Right here in this area would have been the county, after I couldn't go back to [DEFENDANT]; and they wouldn't take me. I tried all of their yards.

Mr. Franklin severely limited his job search to the exact industry he was working in previously. The concrete field is not the only employer that would hire a Class B CDL Truck Driver. Mr. Franklin did not attempt to seek employment from any of the other employers in the area.

The resources Mr. Franklin utilized to find job positions were also severely limited. Individuals seeking employment and performing a diligent job search utilize a combination of methods to search for employment including, electronic job posting boards, job fairs, newspaper want ads, trade industry publications, and word of mouth. Mr. Franklin did not utilize these resources to find replacement employment that were available to him. Mr. Franklin testified to the following:

> **Q:** Did you put together a resume?
> **A:** No. I just went and filled out applications and talked to people.

In fact, there were many job postings on electronic job boards such as Indeed.com and SimplyHired.com seeking individuals with a Class B CDL, of which Mr. Franklin had. The job postings were for jobs that were located in the area and surrounding area near where Mr. Franklin lived. Mr. Franklin did not expand his job search location when seeking employment and Mr. Franklin did not attempt to obtain employment any other way except through in person meetings for job positions that may or may not have been available.

The data further indicates that Mr. Franklin was underemployed in his position as a Factory Worker earning $10.40 per hour. The positions that Mr. Franklin was qualified to hold in Mr. Franklin's LWIA and outside of the LWIA he lived in, typically earned between $14.67 and $26.54. The job position that Mr. Franklin obtained had earnings less than what he was capable of earning. The BLS occupational handbook did not list Factory Worker as a similar position to Truck Driver. The BLS OOH utilizes job responsibilities, skills, educational requirements, certifications, and training requirements to determine similar jobs. Factory Worker or another similar labor intensive factory job was not identified as requiring similar skills or other factors utilized by the BLS OOH.

Based on research and data, it was found that Mr. Franklin's period of unemployment was not consistent with the demand that existed for his job position and region. Mr. Franklin was unemployed for several years. Data from the BLS CPS indicated that Mr. Franklin could have found a replacement job position within 12–29 weeks following a diligent search, and not the more than three years Mr. Franklin was unemployed. The expected duration of unemployment was based on Mr. Franklin's occupation, similar occupations, and geographic location had he performed a diligent search. As research suggests, these positions Mr. Franklin would have been qualified to apply and hold would have provided Mr. Franklin with similar wages to those that he received as a Truck Driver previously.

Case Study 3: Fire Fighters' Association v. The City

Abstract This case study utilizes a compensation analysis to determine whether public sector employees earned similar compensation to their private sector counterparts. Unlike wages in the private sector, public sector wages are subject to budgetary constraints, and often determined years in advance by collective bargaining agreements. The Plaintiff in this case was a public sector employee union representing firefighters, which sued the city after their prior collective bargaining agreement expired. The Plaintiff sued for back pay and compensation substantially equal to comparable private sector firefighters.

Keywords City workers pay · Union employees · Functional job analysis · Compensation analysis · Bargaining unit

In Brief

This case study utilizes a compensation analysis to determine whether public sector employees earned similar compensation to their private sector counterparts. Unlike wages in the private sector, public sector wages are subject to budgetary constraints, and often determined years in advance by collective bargaining agreements. The Plaintiff in this case was

© The Author(s), under exclusive license to Springer Nature Switzerland AG 2022
D. Steward, *Economic Losses and Mitigation after an Employment Termination*,
https://doi.org/10.1007/978-3-030-88364-5_11

a public sector employee union representing firefighters, which sued the city after their prior collective bargaining agreement expired. The Plaintiff sued for back pay and compensation substantially equal to comparable private sector firefighters.

The equivalent job analysis performed in this case found that firefighters in this city earned a salary comparable, if not higher, than an equivalent private sector worker.

Background

The Plaintiff in this case was a Professional Fire Fighters Association, a public sector union, for a large municipality. In 2013, the city and the fire fighters' union signed a three year collective bargaining agreement, which expired in 2016. By 2019, the city and union were unable to reach a new agreement. The union filed suit against the city for not properly compensating its firefighters after the collective bargaining agreement expired.

This particular city faces unique statutory requirements for paying police officers and firefighters. Under existing law, the city's firefighters must earn compensation that is substantially equal to prevailing compensation for firefighters in the private sector. Municipal firefighters' compensation, according to the law, must be equivalent to other private sector jobs that require the same or similar skill, abilities, and training.

However, the statute did not specify how to compare the compensation rates of public and private sector firefighters. Exactly what constituted a "comparable" private sector firefighter was open to interpretation. Some private sector firefighters have different skill sets depending on the kinds of fires they fight or facilities they have to protect, thus a direct comparison could be inaccurate. By examining the job duties and requirements of a municipal firefighter, an analysis can be performed by first constructing a private sector equivalent position in this case.

Analysis

In 2015, the fire department conducted an internal analysis of a firefighter's daily tasks. Each job task and responsibility was specifically detailed and categorized by its frequency and relative importance. These included common tasks such as carrying more than 100lbs of equipment, bandaging wounds, driving the fire engine, or extinguishing the sources of fires. But they also include less obvious tasks like communicating with citizens, performing salvage operations, cleaning the station, or participating in continuing firefighting education. There were over 250 different tasks which firefighters were expected to perform.

These tasks and responsibilities were then grouped into general job duty categories, such as Emergency Medical Service Operations, or Rescue Operations. The department identified 15 such job duties, then calculated what percent of a firefighter's time was spent performing each job duty.

Duty Areas		Frequency	Importance	Essentiality
Tactical Duties		**70%**	**65%**	**64%**
1	Emergency Medical Service Operations	23%	20%	18%
2	Hazardous Materials Operations	4%	4%	6%
3	Hoseline and Attack Operations	9%	8%	7%
4	Incident Command	4%	3%	3%
5	Incident Response	6%	7%	8%
6	Ladder Operations	6%	5%	5%
7	Pumping and Driving Operations	7%	7%	6%
8	Rescue Operations	7%	6%	5%
9	Salvage and Overhaul Operations	4%	5%	6%
Non-Tactical Duties		**30%**	**35%**	**36%**
10	Administrative Duties and Communications	4%	4%	5%
11	External and Interagency Collaborations	3%	4%	4%
12	Prevention and Inspections	4%	4%	4%
13	Public Relations and Customer Service	6%	6%	6%
14	Station and Equipment Maintenance	6%	9%	9%
15	Training and Education	7%	8%	8%
Totals		**100%**	**100%**	**100%**

A hypothetical private sector equivalent would tie a monetary value to each of the firefighter's job duties, by calculating the market value of such equivalent services in the local private sector.

The monetary value of each job task or service would then be weighted by the proportion of time a firefighter spends performing the given job duty.

For example, if a private sector employee was paid $50,000/year for a job equivalent to one of the firefighter's job duties, and the firefighter performed that task 10% of the time, the market value of that firefighter's job duty would be $5,000/year. These weighted values would then be aggregated until, finally, a hypothetical private sector equivalent job would be formed.

Comparing a firefighter's specific job duty to a private sector employee requires a detailed description of potentially equivalent jobs, so they could be compared to the tasks and functions of each job duty. One generally accepted and frequently utilized labor market resource is the Bureau of Labor Statistics' Occupational Outlook Handbook (OOH). The OOH provides information on tasks performed by different occupations, the job's work environment, education, training, and qualifications. The OOH also has calculations for pay in a given occupation by different states and regions.

For example, the job description of EMTs and Paramedics within the OOH closely aligned with the Firefighter's Tactical Duties for "Emergency Medical Service Operations", which comprise almost a quarter of the firefighter's time. Similarly, the job description of a Fire Inspector closely aligned with the tasks outlined in "Preventions and Inspections." This same kind of analysis could be made for the firefighter's Non-Tactical Duties: the tasks required for "Public Relations and Customer Service" closely matched the job description of a Public Relations Specialist in the OOH.

Emergency Medical Service Operations Tasks:

1	Prepare and transfer a patient to an emergency vehicle.
2	Control bleeding and bandage wounds.
3	Lift a patient into a bed/onto a stretcher and carry the patient to the emergency vehicle.
4	Assess a patient's condition.
5	Gather information from patients or family regarding medical history.
6	Perform cardiopulmonary resuscitation or other appropriate cardiac emergency procedures.
7	Operate Defibrillator (AED).
8	Properly utilize emergency equipment and supplies.

(continued)

(continued)

Emergency Medical Service Operations Tasks:	
9	Administer appropriate oxygen flow to patients.
10	Monitor and provide.
11	Administer first aid and cardiopulmonary resuscitation to injured persons.
12	Physically control patients who are hysterical, mentally disturbed, or in an altered state of consciousness that require medical attention.
13	Immobilize painful, swollen, or deformed extremities.

Some job duties involved a fusion of multiple jobs: for example, the firefighters's "Hoseline and Attack Operations" mirrored job tasks and work requirements for both Hand Laborers and Pipefitters as found in the OOH. A combination of the two occupation's job skills, and thus wages, would be necessary to calculate the value of the "Hosline and Attack Operations" job duty.

After aligning each job duty with an occupation, the pay rates for each job duty can be calculated by looking at the salary (market value) of the occupation which matches that firefighter job duty. For example, in the metropolitan area where this dispute arose, the average Emergency Medical Technician or Paramedic made about $34,500 per year. So, the firefighters "Emergency Medical Services Operations" could reasonably be estimated to be worth $34,500 per year. About 22–23% of the firefighter's time is spent performing this listed job duty. Therefore, the job task the firefighter would perform could reasonably be said to be worth about $7,700 per year.

After all of these individuals' calculations of salaries and task frequency, the pay rates for each job duty would be aggregated together. The final computed salary would be the market value of this firefighter's services in the local metropolitan area. This final estimate should represent the hypothetical private sector equivalent job, which would closely align with the firefighters actual skills, abilities, and training.

The job task analysis deployed for this case revealed that firefighters in the city earned compensation higher than the equivalent local market value of their services. An equivalent, hypothetical private sector job would have paid a median wage of approximately $46,000 in the local area, with an estimated range of $57,000 in pay from the highest to lowest end. By contrast, the firefighters in the city were being paid a median salary of almost $51,000 annually. Despite the union's claim that the firefighters were underpaid, firefighters in this case actually earned over $5,000 more than the hypothetical private sector equivalent in the local metropolitan area.

This analysis differed sharply from the Plaintiff's expert's analysis in this case. The expert was asked by the Plaintiffs to compare the compensation and condition of employment of members of the firefighters union to private sector employees in the labor market. The expert selected and obtained data on 15 private fire departments to use as comparators, with special focus on 3 private firefighting departments in the state. The opposing expert concluded that the city's firefighters were being paid several thousand dollars lower than private sector firefighters.

However, the Plaintiff's analysis was critically flawed for one reason: many of these private fire departments did not meet the criteria to be an appropriate comparator. Private sector comparators had to be in the same labor market and had to perform under the same working conditions as municipal firefighters. One of the expert's comparators was a private fire company at a radioactive munitions facility. The types of training a firefighter would have to undergo to handle radioactive material, or fires involving radioactive material, are distinctly different from the job duties and working conditions of a typical municipal firefighter.

Other private sector comparators included firefighters working for regional airports outside of the state. Firefighters working for airports have to undergo specific training that supplements, or diverges, from traditional municipal firefighters; airport firefighters have to operate different equipment, use specialized fire suppression techniques, and learn unique evacuation protocols.

The Assistant Fire Chief of the city's Fire Department, in his deposition, insisted that the department explicitly avoided comparing their own salaries to private sector firefighters.

Q: Look on the second page of this affidavit that you had there.
A: Uh-huh.
Q: See down at the bottom, it looks like you made some comments there. Would you read those for me, please?
A: [The City] responds to both medical and fire calls for service [over a broad geographical area]. From my fire service experience, I'm familiar with some aspects of private sector fire employment, including those in refinery and/or industrial sectors. However, based on my knowledge and in the absence of comparators

provided by [the union], I am not aware of a private sector fire employment comparable to fire employment [by the City] with conditions of employment in the labor-market area in other jobs that require the same or similar skills, ability, and training and may be performed under the same or similar conditions. [...]

Q: When you say "comparable," what do you mean in your affidavit?
A: When you -- when you say "fire service comparable," a fire service or fire department that does everything that [our department] does. That's what I mean by that.
Q: Okay.
A: So everything that we're doing, other departments may do; some may not. But in the private sector, they are not going to be responding to calls from the public for service. So in that aspect, they may not be comparable because we're – we're doing a lot.

However, the Assistant Fire Chief readily acknowledged that his own skills as a firefighter could be directly compared to those with a similar skill set in the public or private sector.

Q: Do you consider yourself to be a -- comparable as a firefighter, if we wanted to look at the labor market and figure out what your skills are --
A: Okay.
Q: -- do you think we could compare your skills to the public or private sector?
A: My skills, yeah.

This is why constructing a private sector equivalent job, based on job duties and tasks, proved essential for this case. It would have been insufficient to simply compare employees with the job title "firefighter" in the private sector to employees with the job title "firefighter" in the public sector. What was more important was to determine what tasks and skills constituted a municipal firefighter for this city, and determine what the market value of those skills would be.

This form of compensation analysis is both more realistic in scope, and better satisfies the specific statutory requirements of the state that mandated equivalent compensation for private and public sector firefighters. In this case, it showed that the city's firefighters were more than adequately compensated for their skillset.

The hypothetical private sector comparator is a useful tool to analyze public sector compensation, by analyzing the market value of tasks and skills. However, it is a type of analysis which does raise its own difficult questions.

For example, wages in the private sector are closely tied to the profitability of the specific industry. This may lead to very wide ranges in potential compensation for specific job tasks. Emergency Management Directors (EMDs) have a skillset which is similar to the above "Incident Command" tasks. But the wages of private EMDs may drastically vary depending on the profitability of their industry: Oil & Gas, Aviation, or Healthcare. What is the appropriate range of private sector salaries to consider for the comparator? Salaries in public sector fire departments do not tend to fluctuate drastically.

The mix of job duties among private sector companies, and thus specific occupations, will also vary across industries. For example, the skills of an EMD may be quantified as a section of a firefighter's job tasks. However, the overall mix of job duties of an EMD in a hospital would be different from those of an EMD in a refinery. Is there a sense in which one industry is a better comparator than another when trying to build an equivalent job position based on job tasks?

Finally, there are different budgeting restrictions that public employees face that private sector employees are not subject to. Municipalities have to answer to their constituents and taxpayers, who have competing non-market valuations of public sector salaries. Public sector salaries are subject to available funds, a political decision that is absent in a private sector equivalent. Indeed, if the funds do not exist in the private sector, such jobs would not exist. How should the public sector budget process factor into the calculation of a private sector equivalent?

Case Study 4: Attorney v. Public Utility Employer

Abstract In this case the Plaintiff, Ms. Traci Stevenson, worked for a public utility employer as its General Counsel. Ms. Stevenson alleged she was terminated for discriminatory reasons. Approximately two years after Ms. Stevenson's termination, she obtained employment with a legal staffing agency. An analysis of the Plaintiff's job search efforts and of the labor market for individuals with Ms. Stevenson's knowledge, expertise and skills were performed. It was found that Ms. Stevenson did not perform an adequate job search relative to the job market available to her. Ms. Stevenson's job search was sporadic, inconsistent, and did not accurately represent the opportunities that were available to her. Ms. Stevenson additionally claimed defamation by her employer hindered her employer opportunities. Ms. Stevenson's job search records and deposition testimony from Ms. Stevenson revealed no indication that comments made by her employer had reduced her ability to obtain employment.

Keywords Defamation · Attorney compensation · Contract work

In Brief

In this case the Plaintiff, Ms. Traci Stevenson, worked for a public utility employer as its General Counsel. Ms. Stevenson alleged she was terminated for discriminatory reasons. Approximately two years after Ms. Stevenson's termination, she obtained employment with a legal staffing agency. An analysis of the Plaintiff's job search efforts and of the labor market for individuals with Ms. Stevenson's knowledge, expertise and skills were performed. It was found that Ms. Stevenson did not perform an adequate job search relative to the job market available to her. Ms. Stevenson's job search was sporadic, inconsistent, and did not accurately represent the opportunities that were available to her. Ms. Stevenson additionally claimed defamation by her employer hindered her employer opportunities. Ms. Stevenson's job search records and deposition testimony from Ms. Stevenson revealed no indication that comments made by her employer had reduced her ability to obtain employment.

Background

In this case the Plaintiff, Ms. Traci Stevenson, worked for a public utility employer as its General Counsel. In her position as General Counsel, Ms. Stevenson was responsible for the day-to-day operations of the employer's legal department which included advising the President and CEO, as well as the board and executives of other departments in legal matters. Ms. Stevenson earned $160,000 annually and also received benefits including a pension plan as General Counsel. Ms. Stevenson is a highly educated individual and earned her law degree from a top tier law school. Ms. Stevenson had previously held several positions in law and worked as the owner and principal of a solo practice for approximately three years. Ms. Stevenson had previously held licenses to practice law in multiple states.

Ms. Stevenson alleged she was terminated for discriminatory reasons. Approximately two years after Ms. Stevenson's termination, she obtained employment with a legal staffing agency. In this position Ms. Stevenson received an hourly salary of $25 per hour and did not receive any benefits such as health or life insurance, defined benefit or defined contribution, stock options, and paid vacation.

Analysis

An analysis of the Plaintiff's job search efforts and of the labor market for individuals with Ms. Stevenson's knowledge, expertise and skills were performed. First, it is important to look closely at the job search that the Plaintiff actually performed. This identifies the types of jobs that the Plaintiff believes relates to their work experience and value. In this case, Ms. Stevenson applied for a range of jobs varying in skill level, and job and educational requirements. Among those jobs that Ms. Stevenson applied for was contract work to perform data entry. Ms. Stevenson was overqualified for job positions such as data entry and it is highly unusual for an individual with an advanced degree such as a law degree to perform work with minimum educational requirements.

Many skills Ms. Stevenson possessed were transferable to other occupations that utilized those skills. For instance, an overview of related occupations from the ONET Online system was utilized to identify other potential occupations Ms. Stevenson could have sought employment in addition to General Counsel and Lawyer related positions.

Additional research was performed using job boards such as Indeed, SimplyHired, and GlassDoor. These resources allow users to search for job positions based on job title, keywords, or companies for example. A search on these job boards revealed that there are job openings, outside of General Counsel and Lawyer positions, that prefer candidates that hold a Juris Doctor degree. According to research, these job titles included Director of Lawyer Talent Development, Director of Legal Programs, and Transaction Manager. Job positions such as these would be more suitable for Ms. Stevenson to have sought employment for. Ms. Stevenson would likely experience more success applying for job positions she was more closely qualified for.

Ms. Stevenson's job search is shown below. Ms. Stevenson did not provide a comprehensive spreadsheet or list containing the date she applied for a job position or the job title as would be required by the Texas Workforce Commission to receive unemployment benefits. Ms. Stevenson provided pdf's of job application submissions and email confirmations.

Employer	Position Applied For	Location
Sabre Industries	In House Counsel	Minneapolis, MA
Regions	Funeral Trust Legal Counsel	
City of Atlanta	Deputy General Counsel - Real Estate	Atlanta, GA
Medco	Contract Attorney	Kansas City, KS
Mint Dentistry	General Counsel	Dallas, TX
Cardtronics	Sr. Legal Counsel	
Facebook	Director & Associate General Counsel	New York, NY
Google	Document Review Projects	Houston, TX
Oracle	Corporate Attorney	San Francisco, CA
Total	Managing Counsel	Washington, DC
Robert Half	Data Entry Clerk - Legal	Oklahoma City, OK
Just Energy	Associate General Counsel	Chicago, IL
Simply Safe	Contract Litigation Services	Los Angeles, CA
Legal Staffing Agency	Document Reviewer	Seattle, WA

It is important to note in this matter that Ms. Stevenson's records indicate that her job search began more than five months after her termination as General Counsel. Ms. Stevenson was also searching for jobs outside of her current residence. Ms. Stevenson was applying for job positions in Dallas, Fort Worth, Atlanta, and New York among a number of cities. The job locations that Ms. Stevenson was applying to indicate what job markets would be available for her to apply in. The more locations that Ms. Stevenson applied in, the more job opportunities that were available to her. In total, Ms. Stevenson provided job search records for 73 job positions over the nearly two year time period of her unemployment. On average, Ms. Stevenson applied to fewer than four jobs per month.

Deposition testimony also provided additional information regarding the effort Ms. Stevenson put into supplementing her employment and pay.

> Q: Do you say you do not have a law firm at this time? You're not part of a law firm at this time?
> A: Correct.
> Q: Are you advertising as a law firm or have you requested any type of business as an attorney?
> A: I have applied for jobs if that's what you mean.
> Q: No.

A: I have not advertised for work. I had a domain name -- I purchased the domain name that I had before it had expired but I didn't do anything. I have not advertised so no.

Ms. Stevenson had previously worked in a solo practice prior to obtaining her employment as General Counsel. As deposition testimony revealed, Ms. Stevenson did not attempt to supplement her employment or pay by continuing her solo practice.

Further, Ms. Stevenson did obtain employment nearly two years after her termination. Ms. Stevenson was earning less than one-third of the earnings she received as General Counsel working in a role she was significantly overqualified for. Ms. Stevenson did not continue applying to General Counsel or Lawyer related jobs after she obtained non-comparable employment.

Labor market research and studies further demonstrate the high employer demand for Lawyers. Data tabulations showed that in each month since her termination, there were between 178 and 387 job openings for Lawyers in the Houston area. Further data shows on a given day, the actual job posting, company and job title for Lawyers.

Ms. Stevenson's application records show that she did not apply for even a portion of the jobs that were available to her in her current location. Labor market data indicated that the unemployment rate among lawyers was 70% lower than that of other occupations and that job growth for lawyers was expected to continue to grow.

The salaries associated with the job positions that were available to her were between $173,000 and $221,000. These earnings were found to be comparable to her earnings as General Counsel.

It was found that Ms. Stevenson did not perform an adequate job search relative to the job market available to her. Ms. Stevenson's job search was not focused, inconsistent, and did not accurately represent the opportunities that were available to her. Ms. Stevenson did not take advantage of the potential resources she would have had available to her such as a legal recruiter or through other legal communities. Given the labor market available to Ms. Stevenson, she should have been able to obtain comparable replacement employment within 13–43 weeks of beginning a diligent job search.

In this matter, Ms. Stevenson additionally claimed defamation. Ms. Stevenson claimed that she was actively searching for job opportunities and her searches had been unsuccessful due to the media surrounding the lawsuit she filed. Deposition testimony from Ms. Stevenson revealed no indication that comments made by her previous employer had resulted in her inability to receive employment.

> **Q:** Have you done anything else to mitigate your damages since your termination?
> **A:** I've been attempting to mitigate my damages the entire time. I've been actively looking at other positions -- I haven't gotten anything. I mean, you search my name and this is what comes up.
> **Q:** This lawsuit comes up?
> **A:** Yeah.
> **Q:** Have you received any feedback from a job contact stating that you have not been chosen for a role because of this lawsuit?
> **A:** No.

There was no indication that Ms. Stevenson was unable to obtain employment due to the lawsuit filed.

Case Study 5: Medical Doctor v. Physician Group Partners

Abstract The Plaintiff in this case was an experienced Pathologist with expertise in Blood Bank and Transfusion Medicine, who alleged economic damages due to the cessation of his employment agreement with his business partners. In order to address the Plaintiff's alleged lost earnings, a detailed analysis of all the components of his earnings, as well as an analysis of his future employability must be performed. The labor market and economic damage analysis performed in this case showed that the Plaintiff was highly employable and not economically harmed.

Keywords Partnership · Lost business revenue · Breach of contract · Physician compensation · Variable pay

In Brief

The Plaintiff in this case was an experienced Pathologist with expertise in Blood Bank and Transfusion Medicine, who alleged economic damages due to the cessation of his employment agreement with his business partners. In order to address the Plaintiff's alleged lost earnings, a detailed analysis of all the components of his earnings, as well as an analysis of his future employability must be performed. The labor market and economic damage analysis performed in this case showed that the Plaintiff was highly employable and not economically harmed.

Background

In July 2012, the Plaintiff, Dr. Arnoldo Rasmussen, entered into an associate employment agreement with the defendant to work as a Pathologist. The agreement specified a one year initial term which would automatically renew for successive one year periods unless it was terminated by either party or the parties mutually agreed to renegotiate the Agreement at the end of the initial term. The Agreement also specified various duties, licensure requirements, and Dr. Rasmussen's potential compensation structure.

According to the Agreement, Dr. Rasmussen's potential total compensation, which was referred to as 'Full Compensation' in the Agreement, was to be comprised of a base salary, discretionary incentive bonus and education/auto allowance. The Agreement specified that Dr. Rasmussen's actual annual compensation was to be paid as a percentage of the Full Compensation. The percentage of Full Compensation that was to be paid to Dr. Rasmussen increased over the first three contract years from 30 to 50%.

Dr. Rasmussen's compensation in the fourth and subsequent years was contingent upon being elected to "shareholder status". The Agreement specified that election to shareholder status required an affirmative vote of three-fourths of the existing shareholders. If Dr. Rasmussen was to be elected to shareholder status after three years, Dr. Rasmussen would be eligible to become a shareholder and to purchase 9,000 shares from the defendant. Dr. Rasmussen received income from the defendant employer of $101,892, $306,655 and $375,948 in the years 2012, 2013, and 2014 respectively.

Prior to his employment at the defendant, Dr. Rasmussen's tax returns indicate that he was employed as a Physician in two major metropolitan areas. Working as a resident Physician during 2010 and 2011, Dr. Rasmussen earned $530,454 and $512,712, respectively.

Dr. Rasmussen's self-reported employment history shows that he has regained employment in some capacities since his termination. According to Dr. Rasmussen's LinkedIn profile, he has worked as a Medical Director and Corporate Medical Consultant for several organizations since his employment at the defendant ended. Dr. Rasmussen's profile indicates that since June 2015 he has worked as a Medical Director for four different organizations. Dr. Rasmussen also worked as a Corporate Medical Consultant for one organization according to his LinkedIn profile.

Documents produced by the Plaintiff further indicate that Dr. Rasmussen has been in the process of establishing an independent pathology practice. The Plaintiff's records show that at least as early as March 2016, Dr. Rasmussen was working with a medical consulting firm to establish an independent medical practice. According to the initial business plan, the medical consulting firm was working with Dr. Rasmussen to establish an on-site pathology practice.

Analysis

Under his employment agreement with the defendant, the Plaintiff's earnings were composed of compensation, such as incentive payments, that was not guaranteed and could vary from year to year. Dr. Rasmussen's compensation agreement clearly states that the incentive bonus component of his compensation was discretionary and not guaranteed. The Agreement defines the incentive bonuses as "the bonuses, if any, that may be payable quarterly or at more frequent intervals as determined by the Association in amounts determined at the discretion of the Association." It is economically reasonable to project that any incentive bonus could be higher in some years, lower in other years, or not awarded at all in a given year.

Further, a large component of Dr. Rasmussen's potential earnings with the defendant hinged on whether he would be elected to shareholder status after three years of employment with the defendant. According to Dr. Rasmussen's employment agreement, if Dr. Rasmussen would have received the necessary three-fourths vote from shareholders, he would have been eligible to purchase CPA shares. If Dr. Rasmussen were to be elected to shareholder status, then the cost of these shares would need to be deducted appropriately from his alleged economic losses.

Dr. Rasmussen's compensation agreement clearly indicates the election to shareholder status is not guaranteed. In fact, The Agreement provides several employment options in the event that Dr. Rasmussen is not elected to shareholder status. The Agreement, as shown below, details the possible scenarios in which an employee does not become an elected shareholder.

(f) If Pathologist does not become eligible to become a shareholder of the Association in accordance with Section 2.07(a), the Association, in its sole discretion may either (i) terminate Pathologist's employment upon sixty days written notice, (ii) offer Pathologist continued employment as an Associate Pathologist, with compensation to be determined by the Association, or (iii) offer Pathologist employment in a capacity other than Associate or Shareholder.

In order to perform an economically sound analysis of Dr. Rasmussen's alleged lost earnings, it is necessary to account for generally accepted economic possibilities, such as the possibility that the incentive bonus amount may change (or not be paid at all) in a given year, the possibility that Dr. Rasmussen does not achieve shareholder status, or the possibility that Dr. Rasmussen would chose at some point to pursue opportunities outside of the Physician Group partnership.

Further, labor market studies indicate that Dr. Rasmussen is highly employable. It is general labor market knowledge that the labor demand for medical doctors, including Pathologists, is high statewide and nationwide. The unemployment rate of medical doctors is consistently, and substantially, lower than that of other professionals.

If Dr. Rasmussen were to perform an adequate job search he could be expected to regain comparable employment within a reasonable period of time. Pathologists with the knowledge, skills and abilities possessed by Dr. Rasmussen are in high demand. Even a casual review of labor market data and popular electronic job posting boards such as CareerMD.com, Indeed.com, and PracticeLink.com show that there are currently job openings for individuals with Dr. Rasmussen's background. Given his work history and training, Dr. Rasmussen would have been at least minimally qualified to hold any number of these positions. These types of job postings indicate only a portion of the employer demand that exists for Dr. Rasmussen's job skills, since not all job openings are necessarily reflected. Some job openings in a geographic area are advertised through trade industry publications, and word of mouth networking.

At the time that Dr. Rasmussen resigned from the Physician Group Partnership, there were employers of various sizes in the San Antonio metropolitan area that had openings for pathologists. U.S. Bureau of Labor Statistics ("BLS") data tabulations and pathologist labor market data indicate that there were at least 20 pathologist job position openings in a typical month in 2014 in his metropolitan statistical area. Dr.

Rasmussen would have been qualified to apply for any number of these positions.

The typical wages associated with these pathologist job positions is comparable to the compensation that Dr. Rasmussen earned with the defendant. Labor market salary data for pathologists show that Dr. Rasmussen could conservatively be expected to earn an average salary of at least $347,000 in private practice. It is likely that Dr. Rasmussen's education, specializations, and knowledge would demand a higher than average salary from replacement employers.

Further, Dr. Rasmussen could have been expected to obtain a job position that was comparable to the one he held at the partnership within a reasonable period of time if he would have performed a sufficient replacement employment job search. Overall, the unemployment rate of medical doctors including Pathologists is consistently, and substantially, lower than that of other professionals. Labor market data from the BLS indicate that Dr. Rasmussen could have reasonably been expected to obtain employment within approximately 26–29 weeks of beginning a sufficiently thorough and diligent job search following his resignation from the partnership. If Dr. Rasmussen would have performed a sufficient job search immediately following his resignation, it is likely that his experience and expertise would have given him an advantage over many job candidates and shortened his replacement job search time. Dr. Rasmussen's labor market employability and demand for his services would likely be further enhanced in private practice. In any event, Dr. Rasmussen could have reasonably been expected to find comparable replacement employment within the approximate 100 week period that spans from the date of his resignation to the date of this analysis.

Further, Plaintiff produced documents which showed he was starting his own practice. Not seeking other employment that could provide him benefits if he was to become self-employed. It would also involve taking on additional expenses which could potentially lower his expected income, especially in the firm's start-up years of operation.

Case Study 6: CFO v. Fintech Employer

Abstract In this case study, we provide an example of a Plaintiff in an employment termination lawsuit who was employed as the Chief Financial Officer of a well-known firm in the financial sector. Due to her termination, the Plaintiff alleges that she incurred economic damages which included not only her base salary and incentive compensation, but also compensation under a phantom stock program. As will be discussed, there are numerous components of an executive's economic damage calculation that must be appropriately taken into account, such as not only the availability of executive-level jobs in the Plaintiff's labor market, but also the underlying elements of the employer phantom stock program and other forms of incentive compensation.

Keywords Phantom stock compensation plan · Fintech Industry · Executive compensation · Performance bonuses

In Brief

In this case study, we provide an example of a Plaintiff in an employment termination lawsuit who was employed as the Chief Financial Officer of a well-known firm in the financial sector. Due to her termination, the

Plaintiff alleges that she incurred economic damages which included not only her base salary and incentive compensation, but also compensation under a phantom stock program. As will be discussed, there are numerous components of an executive's economic damage calculation that must be appropriately taken into account, such as not only the availability of executive-level jobs in the Plaintiff's labor market, but also the underlying elements of the employer phantom stock program and other forms of incentive compensation.

Background

Prior to her termination, the Plaintiff, Ms. Angela Maroney, was employed as the Chief Technology Officer (CTO) of a consumer financial services company. As CTO, Ms. Maroney was responsible for the product development and operations of her division and all of its underlying properties. At the time of her termination, Ms. Maroney earned a base salary of $260,000, and was also eligible to receive annual bonuses and equity grants.

The company provided the Plaintiff with annual bonus compensation that was an incentive payment equal to a predetermined percentage of her salary, and was based on company performance. Additionally, the Plaintiff was set to potentially receive equity grants in the form of phantom shares of the company's stock. A phantom stock plan is a deferred compensation plan that provides the employee an award measured by the value of the employer's common stock. However, unlike actual stock, the award does not confer equity ownership in the company. In other words, there is no actual stock given to the employee. The value of Ms. Maroney's equity grant compensation was subject to many factors, including job tenure and satisfactory job performance.

Within a month after her employment at the defendant employer was terminated, Ms. Maroney obtained an unpaid position as CTO for a startup firm. Ms. Maroney testified that she worked in the unpaid CTO position for approximately four months, but left the company after they failed to obtain funding. After a few months of unemployment, Ms. Maroney was hired as Chief Information Officer for another company in the financial industry.

ANALYSIS

Due to the complicated nature of the Plaintiff's compensation package as an executive, each component of the Plaintiff's wages needed to be appropriately addressed. The structure of the Plaintiff's incentive compensation, both the bonuses and equity grants, were outlined in a memo that the company's Chief Financial Officer provided to the Plaintiff shortly after the company went through some restructuring. This memorandum projected the Plaintiff's possible earnings at the defendant employer over a five year period. However, while the structure of the compensation was promised to the Plaintiff had she remained employed, the specific payment amounts listed in the memo were hypothetical and did not accurately reflect the earnings that the Plaintiff could actually expect to receive.

	2019	2020	2021	2022	2023
Base	$260,000	$260,000	$260,000	$260,000	$260,000
MIP Target - 36% of base	$93,600	$93,600	$93,600	$93,600	$93,600
Cash Compensation	$353,600	$353,600	$353,600	$353,600	$353,600
Equity Value					
Number of Vested Units	339	960	1,815	2,333	2,569
Value per Unit	$339.48	$407.38	$488.85	$586.63	$703.95
Equity Value - Current Year	$115,084	$276,001	$496,178	$481,345	$439,840
Total Equity Value - End of Year		$391,085	$887,263	$1,368,608	$1,808,448
Total Annual Compensation	$468,684	$629,601	$849,778	$834,945	$793,440

According the Plaintiff's compensation memo, over the period of 2019 to 2023, her salary would remain unchanged at $260,000, and she would be eligible for bonus compensation (referred to as MIP Target - Management Incentive Plan) equal up to 36% of her base salary, or a maximum of $93,600 per year. While there were no specific company policies that were provided during the Discovery phase of this case, deposition testimony from the Person Most Knowledgeable (PMK) at the company indicated that the full bonus amount was not a guaranteed payment.

Q: But what Exhibit No. 12 indicates is that Ms. Maroney was expected to have a base salary of $260,000 annually for 2019 through 2023; is that right?
A: Yes.
Q: And that she was expected to have a bonus for 2019 through 2023, each year, of $93,600; is that accurate?
A: That's the target for the bonus, correct.
Q: Right. And do you have any reason to believe that that target would not have been obtained?
A: The bonus would have been based on her performance, so I don't know what that would have been, so I -- I can't confirm these exact amounts. It's not guaranteed that she would get $93,600 every year.

Additionally, the memo provided that the Plaintiff could receive equity grant compensation that was subject to a three year vesting schedule. As detailed in the memo, at the end of the first quarter of each specified year, the Plaintiff would receive a grant of a certain number of phantom stock units equal to $300,000 in value.

Under a phantom stock plan, employers promise to pay their employees a cash bonus based on the gained value of the phantom units at the end of the vesting period. Although similar to a normal stock plan, in a phantom stock plan the employee does not actually receive a stake in the company, just a virtual placeholder of sorts. Depending on the plan type, at the end of the vesting period the employee will either receive the full value of the grant or strictly the appreciation in the value from the grant date.

In the Plaintiff's case, she was eligible to receive the full value of the $300,000 equity grant and any appreciation at the end of a three year vesting period. At the end of each year in the three year period, one-third of the Plaintiff's equity grant would vest, and she would receive a cash payment equal to the current value of the company's shares. The above memo indicates that at the time of vesting, the shares will be paid at the actual share value, however the example compensation that it describes very optimistically assumes that Ms. Maroney's shares would appreciate at 20% per year. It is crucial to use actual share prices when attempting to value an employee's stock plan, as using overstated assumptions such as a 20% return would be economically unsound.

Generally accepted and peer reviewed research suggests that there are factors that must be considered when evaluating an employee's unrealized stock compensation. Ms. Maroney's stock based compensation was subject to many factors, including the company's financial performance, stock market fluctuations, job tenure, vesting rules, and satisfactory performance in her job. It is a well established and uncontroversial fact that a company's stock price is subject to fluctuations that causes their underlying stock price to increase or decrease over any given time period. In reality, the company's actual stock price has not historically grown anywhere near the 20% assumed in the CFO's memo. As just one of the factors, the historical stock price must be considered when attempting to project the value of the company's stock in the future.

On the other side of the Plaintiff's mitigation analysis, the employee's re-employment prospects are considered. The job search of a c-suite executive differs from the job search of a typical employee, and therefore calls for a tailor made labor market analysis. However, in this case, labor market studies of post employment termination job search efforts have found that the majority of managerial workers find comparable replacement employment that paid as much or more than they previously earned within less time than Ms. Maroney's experienced period of unemployment.

It is often the case that executives will engage the services of an executive search firm to assist with the job search process, as well as rely on deep networks that they have developed over their career. In fact, Ms. Maroney testified that she actually found both of her post-termination jobs as CFO and CIO through her networking connections.

Q: And how did you get that job?
A: Right around - right after my termination I spoke to -- I called Barry Hughes and started talking to him. And he was going to be starting -- he was going to be working on an idea. And so he asked me if I would be the CTO for his startup.
Q: Okay. And what have you done since you left the startup?
A: I'm actually networking and in the process of securing a job with a company.

A further examination of the employer demand for individuals with Ms. Maroney's expertise showed that there were job openings that she would have been qualified to apply for employment. According to job openings data from the State Workforce Commission there are numerous job openings for positions Ms. Maroney would have been qualified to hold. For example, in her geographic area there were openings for Computer and Information Systems Manager and Chief Executives in the month of Ms. Maroney's termination. The engagement of an executive search firm would in all likelihood increase the number of employment opportunities that were available to Ms. Maroney. Had Ms. Maroney performed a sufficient job search, any number of these job positions would have been available to an individual with Ms. Maroney's knowledge, skills and expertise.

In fact, labor market data indicates that Ms. Maroney could have found reasonable comparable employment and received earnings comparable to the earnings she received with the Defendant had she performed a sufficiently diligent job search. As mentioned above, Ms. Maroney has been unemployed or in a position that did not offer compensation for more than one and a half years from the date of her termination at the Defendant. Tabulations from the U.S. Bureau of Labor Statistics (BLS) Current Population Survey (CPS) indicate that an individual with Ms. Maroney's experience can be expected to obtain comparable replacement employment within a shorter time period. CPS data indicates that individuals with Ms. Maroney's employment background could reasonably be expected to regain comparable replacement employment within approximately 31 weeks of beginning a sufficiently diligent job search.

The typical wages associated with many of these positions is comparable to the compensation that Ms. Maroney earned in her employment with the Defendant. As mentioned, Ms. Maroney's annual salary was $260,000 at the time her employment ended. According to salary reports from the Society for Human Resource Management (SHRM), an individual in a Chief Technology Officer position in Austin, Texas in the Financial Services industry could expect an average annual salary of approximately $269,700. The data also shows that target bonus percentages for these individuals is comparable to the target bonus Ms. Maroney received at the Defendant. It is also common for individuals working in these positions to receive stock grants or options that are comparable to the equity grants that Ms. Maroney received.

The Plaintiff in this case elected to forego her job search by accepting an unpaid position at a start-up company in the financial industry, with hopes that it would ultimately pay off. However, after four months without pay, the Plaintiff left the company in search of a paid executive position. Although the Plaintiff spent the next few months unemployed, she testified that she actually found replacement employment with comparable compensation to her pre-termination earnings within just a week or two of leaving the unpaid position at the start-up firm. According to the Plaintiff, she previously signed a contract with the defendant employer prohibiting her employment at her replacement employer for a specified period of time, which caused her extended period of unemployment until the contract expired.

Case Study 7: VP of Business Development v. Energy Company

Abstract In this lawsuit, the Plaintiff alleged that her position as Vice President of the Midstream Sector of a large oil and gas company was wrongfully terminated, and as a result she has incurred economic damages in the range of $4–5 million. The Plaintiff alleged that she experienced economic damages of lost wages, retirement benefits, and stock compensation. Due to the complex nature of the Plaintiff's employment as an executive in the Oil & Gas industry, advanced economic models reflecting the Plaintiff's compensation and labor market opportunities were formulated and used to assess the Plaintiff's allegations.

Keywords Executive compensation · Oil and gas industry · Job openings data · Headhunters · Midstream · SHRM salary data

In Brief

In this lawsuit, the Plaintiff alleged that her position as Vice President of the Midstream Sector of a large oil and gas company was wrongfully terminated, and as a result she has incurred economic damages in the range of $4–5 million. The Plaintiff alleged that she experienced economic damages of lost wages, retirement benefits, and stock compensation. Due to the complex nature of the Plaintiff's employment as an executive in the Oil & Gas industry, advanced economic models reflecting the Plaintiff's compensation and labor market opportunities were formulated and used to assess the Plaintiff's allegations.

Background

The Plaintiff, Ms. Carol Baskin, was employed as the Vice President of the Midstream Sector at the time her employment at the Defendant employer was terminated. As Vice President of Midstream, Ms. Baskin was in charge of generating business opportunities and revenue for the defendant's midstream business. In the Oil & Gas industry, the midstream sector relates to the transportation, storage, and wholesale marketing of the product, whether that is petroleum or natural gas. Ms. Baskin's annual base salary at the time of her termination was $255,000.

Ms. Baskin was also eligible to participate in the Defendant's Incentive Compensation plans. The Defendant provided a copy of Ms. Baskin's offer letter which detailed the compensation that Ms. Baskin was eligible to earn as Vice President of Midstream. Ms. Baskin had the potential to earn annual bonuses and stock-based compensation that was tied to the company's successful achievement of certain business units and company financial targets and goals. The value of Ms. Baskin's stock-based compensation was subject to many factors, including the company's performance, stock market fluctuations, job tenure and vesting, and satisfactory job performance. Ms. Baskin also received standard employer fringe benefits including medical and dental insurance, and retirement benefits.

Prior to her employment as a Vice President of Midstream, Ms. Baskin worked as a Vice President of Business Development for the Defendant from approximately November 2014 to August 2016. Prior to working for the Defendant, Ms. Baskin worked as the Director of Business Development and Vice President of Business Development for a major energy infrastructure company from 2008 to 2014. Ms. Baskin's resume and deposition testimony indicated that she had over 15 years of high-level employment experience in the Oil and Gas industry.

> Q: Okay. This is Exhibit 1, as I mentioned. This is, I believe a copy of your resume.
> A: Yes.
> Q: Okay. And is this an accurate and current copy of your resume?

A: Yes.
Q: Okay. And you describe yourself, Ms. Baskin, as a result-driven and forward-thinking energy executive who has extensive experience, with over 15 years in leadership, marketing, lobbying, acquisitions, pipeline expansions, business development and operations. Is that a fair summary of your experience and expertise?
A: I believe so.

At the time of her deposition, Ms. Baskin testified that she applied for six job positions that were comparable to the employment she held at the Defendant. Since her employment ended almost two years ago, in February 2018, Ms. Baskin has applied for approximately 14 job positions that were comparable to the employment she held at the Defendant.

DATE (approx.)	POSITION APPLIED
Apr-18	Vice President of Business Development
Jun-20	Vice President of Commercial
Oct-20	Vice President of Customer Service
Jan-20	Vice President and General Manager - C&I
Jan-20	Director - Business Development
Jan-20	Vice President of Marketing
Mar-19	Director - Business Development
Dec-19	Director of Business Dev
Dec-19	Business Development Director
Dec-19	Vice President of Marketing and Sales
Dec-19	Director of Government Affairs
Jan-20	Director of Operations
Jan-20	State & Local Government Affairs Director
Jan-20	Vice President of Gas Utility Operations

Ms. Baskin found replacement employment outside of the Oil and Gas industry in a non-executive level position. Ms. Baskin is currently employed as the Operations Director with a local non-profit. Ms. Baskin currently earns an annual salary of $70,000 in her employment at the non-profit.

Analysis

The analysis of Ms. Baskin's alleged damages resulting from her employment termination is performed by first projecting her future employability after her separation from the defendant. As mentioned above, Ms. Baskin found post-termination employment working as the Operations Director at her church. Ms. Baskin is underemployed in this position that is outside of the Oil & Gas industry. However, had Ms. Baskin conducted a consistent and diligent job search following her employment termination, it is likely that she would have been able to obtain comparable replacement employment within a reasonable period of time.

It is generally accepted that an individual's job search effort is a key factor for success in finding comparable replacement employment. Studies of worker displacement have found that the large majority of managerial workers find comparable replacement employment that paid as much or more as they previously earned, within one year or less. In the two year period following Ms. Baskin's termination, she applied to approximately 14 job positions that were comparable to the position she held at the defendant employer. Further, Ms. Baskin testified at her deposition, which took place about 20 months after her termination, that she had not engaged an executive search firm following the termination of her employment with the defendant employer.

In part due to the particular nature of the work and experiences of individuals in high level executive job positions, it is common for individuals who are actively and diligently searching for comparable employment to engage specialized executive search firms to assist them in their search. In fact, a company representative for the defendant employer testified that in her experience, top level executives typically seek employment through executive recruiting firms. She further stated that candidates can attract the attention of executive search firms through many avenues including severance or placement assistance, networking opportunities, industry and professional organization, and through individual engagement. Executive search firms are compensated on the successful placement of job candidates. Accordingly, high salary earners, like Ms. Baskin, would be an attractive candidate for an executive search firm. Furthermore, many job seekers will work with multiple executive search firms to maximize the likelihood of obtaining their desired job position.

In these types of cases, vocational experts can also be a reliable resource for projecting the Plaintiff's future employability. Both the Plaintiff and the defendant retained the services of vocational experts in this case. The Plaintiff's vocational expert stated in their report that Ms. Baskin had gained valuable transferable skills through her career, and indicated that Ms. Baskin could have been expected to earn more than she currently earns working at her church, and could possibly obtain a job that has a salary in the range of what she made working for the defendant employer. On the other hand, the defendant's vocational expert opined that based on Ms. Baskin's past experience and positions, she could earn upwards of $200,000 in total compensation, which is comparable to what she earned at the defendant employer.

Examination of the employer demand for individuals with the expertise that Ms. Baskin possessed shows that there were job openings that she should have been qualified to apply for employment. In her report, the Plaintiff's vocational expert identified job positions that Ms. Baskin could hold such as Labor Relations Manager, Director (Contract Specialist), and Association Executive. According to job openings data from the Texas Workforce Commission, there are numerous job openings for the positions the vocational expert describes in her report. For example, in her geographical area there were over 250 openings for these types of jobs in the month following Ms. Baskin's termination.

The typical wages associated with many of these positions is comparable to the compensation that Ms. Baskin earned in her employment with the defendant. As mentioned, Ms. Baskin's annual salary was $255,000 in 2017, the last full year of her employment with the defendant. According to salary reports from the Society for Human Resource Management (SHRM), an individual in a Vice President position in her geographical region in the oil and gas industry could expect an annual salary of approximately $313,500. The data also shows that incentive compensation for these individuals is comparable to the amount that Ms. Baskin received at the defendant employer.

In short, there is demand in the market for someone with Ms. Baskin's knowledge, expertise, and experience. If Ms. Baskin were to have performed a sufficient job search, she could have been expected to obtain a job position comparable to the one she held in the energy industry within a reasonable period of time following her termination.

Case Study 8: Duncan v. The City

Abstract In this case, Mr. George Duncan alleges that a criminal trespass letter that his previous employer, 'The City', issued has caused him to incur economic damages. I understand that Mr. Duncan alleges that the criminal trespass letter incident has resulted in the loss of a job position and hindered his employment opportunities. Dr. Rodrick Davis, the Plaintiff's economic expert, opines that Mr. Duncan has incurred a loss of $242,597 in back and front pay. Both Dr. Davis and Dr. Harry Neumann, the Plaintiff's vocational expert, assert that the criminal trespass letter incident will negatively impact Duncan's earnings for at least the next five and a half years. This provides an economic and labor market analysis and a response to the Plaintiff's experts Drs. Davis and Neumann.

Keywords Defamation · Damage to reputation · Email analysis · Vocational expert

In Brief

In this case, Mr. George Duncan alleges that a criminal trespass letter that his previous employer, 'The City', issued has caused him to incur

© The Author(s), under exclusive license to Springer Nature Switzerland AG 2022
D. Steward, *Economic Losses and Mitigation after an Employment Termination*,
https://doi.org/10.1007/978-3-030-88364-5_16

economic damages. I understand that Mr. Duncan alleges that the criminal trespass letter incident has resulted in the loss of a job position and hindered his employment opportunities. Dr. Rodrick Davis, the Plaintiff's economic expert, opines that Mr. Duncan has incurred a loss of $242,597 in back and front pay. Both Dr. Davis and Dr. Harry Neumann, the Plaintiff's vocational expert, assert that the criminal trespass letter incident will negatively impact Duncan's earnings for at least the next five and a half years. This provides an economic and labor market analysis and a response to the Plaintiff's experts Drs. Davis and Neumann.

An analysis of the labor market shows that Mr. Duncan has incurred little to no economic loss in this case. As will be discussed, Drs. Davis and Neumann substantially overstate Mr. Duncan's pre-incident earnings potential at The City. The job position Mr. Duncan states was denied as a result of the letter incident did not have the earnings potential that Drs. Davis and Neumann projected in their reports. Drs. Davis and Neumann's economic damage projections are further inflated by their understatement of Mr. Duncan's current earnings potential. Mr. Duncan could have been and can now be expected to obtain a job position that is comparable to the one at issue in this case within a reasonably short period of time.

Background

It is my understanding that in this lawsuit, Mr. Duncan alleges that the criminal trespass letter City issued to him on August 31, 2012 has resulted in the loss of a job position and hindered his employment opportunities. Mr. Duncan asserts that The City criminal trespass letter resulted in his loss of a temporary employment placement with K-Starr Personnel Agency ('K-Starr'). The K-Starr employment placement would have involved Mr. Duncan working in a non-managerial temporary position as a Contract Coordinator at City Public Works Department.

The Plaintiff's experts Drs. Davis and Neumann provide an analysis of Mr. Duncan's alleged economic damages. Dr. Davis opines that Mr. Duncan has incurred a loss of $242,597 in back and front pay. Dr. Davis projects that but-for the actions of City, Mr. Duncan would have been employed as a Contract Coordinator at the City Public Works Department for at least seven years with starting annual salary of $48,560.

Dr. Davis further projects Mr. Duncan would have earned annual merit increases of 3.0% per year and received City-paid fringe benefits equal to approximately 16% of his annual salary. Dr. Davis projects that over the next seven years, Mr. Duncan would have earned an annual total salary and fringe benefits from the City Public Works Department ranging from $56,330 to $69,136. Dr. Neumann provides a similar opinion concerning Mr. Duncan pre-incident earnings potential at the City Public Works Department.

Both Drs. Davis and Neumann opine that the criminal trespass letter incident will negatively impact Mr. Duncan's future earnings. Drs. Neumann and Davis opine that Mr. Duncan's future earnings will be impacted for up to five and a half and seven years, respectively. According to Drs. Davis and Neumann, Mr. Duncan had applied for job positions in San Antonio, Austin, and Washington D.C. Drs. Davis and Neumann project that Mr. Duncan will now only be able to work as a procurement clerk in the San Antonio area with a projected annual salary of $38,500.

Mr. Duncan's Pre-Incident Employment History

In the six years prior to The City letter incident, Mr. Duncan worked in six different job positions for different employers. Mr. Duncan was employed for approximately two months as a Contract Coordinator for the City Fire Department from approximately December 2011 to February 2012. As a Contract Coordinator, Mr. Duncan's job duties included coordinating contract initiation, monitoring and compliance activities for the City Fire Department. Mr. Duncan resigned from his position in February 2012 following the occurrence of workplace and job performance related issues.

From August 2011 to December 2011, Mr. Duncan was employed as a Temporary Contract Coordinator for the City Fire Department. Mr. Duncan was employed for seven months as Temporary Contract Coordinator for the River Authority from September 2010 to April 2011. Prior to his temporary position, Mr. Duncan was employed for 30 months at Capital Improvement Management Services (CIMS) for the City, 26 months at Lucas Computers, and five months with the County Department of Housing and Human Services. Mr. Duncan's resume indicates he worked at CIMS as a Contract Coordinator from February 2008 to August 2010, Lucas Computers as a Digital Security Specialist from November 2005 to February 2008, and at County Department of Housing and Human Services as a Consultant. Since the letter incident, Mr. Duncan indicates that in addition to his job search he is also involved in an internet venture and the establishment of a Political Action Committee (PAC).

Analysis

Drs. Davis and Neumann overstate Mr. Duncan's City earnings potential. As is discussed in this section, the actual salary and benefits associated with the temporary job that Mr. Duncan alleges that he lost as a result of the letter incident are not consistent with Drs. Davis and Neumann's conjectures. In fact, the job was a temporary position and with a third party employment agency, not The City.

Specifically, Drs. Davis and Neumann overstate the potential earnings associated with the job that Mr. Duncan alleges he lost as a result of The City letter. The City Public Works Department Contract Coordinator job at issue was a temporary job placement through the K-Starr. If Mr. Duncan would have received the temporary job placement, he would have been employed by K-Starr and would not have received salary, health insurance, retirement or any employer paid fringe benefits from City.

In contrast to Drs. Davis and Neumann's assumptions, there was no guarantee that Mr. Duncan's temporary job position at K-Starr would have turned into actual employment at City Public Works. If a permanently funded position were to arise at the City Public Works Department, it would not be guaranteed that the position would go to Mr. Duncan. I have been informed that Mr. Duncan would have had to apply, interview, and be selected for the position if it were to arise. I understand that many internal and external qualified individuals apply for these types of positions at City. It is unreasonable for Drs. Davis and Neumann to assume with complete certainty that Mr. Duncan would have been selected over all other qualified applicants.

Dr. Davis's future salary increase conjectures further inflates the alleged economic losses in this case. Dr. Davis projects that Mr. Duncan would have received a 3.0% annual merit increase each and every year of Mr. Duncan's hypothetical City employment. As mentioned, there was no guarantee that Mr. Duncan's temporary job position at K-Starr would have turned into actual employment at the City Public Works Departments. Further, City's actual pay scale and increase policies do not dictate that Mr. Duncan would have automatically received a 3.0% merit increase in each and every year for seven years. In some recent years the City did not provide merit increases at all to its employees. Dr. Davis's salary increase projections are inappropriate.

The problems with Drs. Davis and Neumann's earnings projections are compounded by Dr. Davis's unrealistic employment tenure assumptions for Mr. Duncan. As mentioned, Dr. Davis's damage analysis assumes that 'but-for' The City letter incident, Mr. Duncan would have been employed in the City Public Works Department position at City for at least eight years from 2012 to at least 2019. Dr. Davis's assumption is inconsistent with Mr. Duncan's actual employment history.

In contrast to Dr. Davis's assumption, Mr. Duncan has no actual history of working at a single job position or employer for anywhere near that length of time. For instance, prior to the letter incident Mr. Duncan worked in six different job positions for different employers. Mr. Duncan worked as a Consultant for the County Department of Housing and Human Services for approximately five months. In this job position, Mr. Duncan indicated in his testimony at the Preliminary Injunction Hearing in this case that his job performance resulted in an early termination of his contract. Mr. Duncan testified:

Q: Did you fill out – did you stay for the entire length of your contract?
A: I don't remember. I don't think so, but I don't remember.
Q: Okay and is the reason that you didn't stay for your entire contract because you didn't get along with people?
A: No, it was not because I didn't get along with people. It's – I don't totally remember why I didn't do it. I think it was probably just because they didn't think I was doing a good job, so --
Q: They didn't think you were doing a good job, and you disagreed with them?
A: No, I didn't disagree with them. I didn't care. I figured it is a subcontract. I am moving on with my life. I got some money to hold me over while I look for a new job, and I didn't care.

Since June 2005, Mr. Duncan's job history indicates that on average he works in a job position for approximately one year, or about 12.6 months. Over the same time period, Mr. Duncan's job history indicates that on average he works for a single employer for approximately one year and three months, or about 15.1 months. Dr. Davis's conjectures are clearly inconsistent with Mr. Duncan's actual work history.

Dr. Davis's conjectures are also inconsistent with conventional, generally accepted labor market data. Mr. Duncan's average job tenure of approximately one year to one year and three months is significantly less than half of the average job tenure in the U.S. Labor market data from the U.S. Bureau of Labor Statistics (BLS) show that the average length of time at one employer for employees similarly situated to Mr. Duncan is approximately 5.67 years (See no. 19 in Exhibit A). Mr. Duncan's actual average job tenure length is significantly less than public employees with Master's degrees. In short, Mr. Duncan's actual employment history does not suggest that he would have been employed at City Public Works Department for the length of time conjectured by Dr. Davis.

Drs. Davis and Neumann understate Mr. Duncan's current earnings potential. Drs. Davis and Neumann's overstated City earnings assumptions are exacerbated by their understatement of Mr. Duncan's current earnings potential. As will be discussed in this section, Drs. Davis and Neumann assumptions concerning Mr. Duncan's job search and job opportunities are unrealistic and inappropriate. In contrast to Drs. Davis and Neumann's conjectures, if Mr. Duncan were to actively and diligently seek replacement employment he could be expected to obtain a job position that is comparable to the job at issue in this case within a reasonably short period of time.

As discussed previously, Drs. Davis and Neumann opine that The City letter incident will negatively impact Mr. Duncan's future earnings for up to five and a half and seven years, respectively. According to their reports, Mr. Duncan states that he has applied for job positions in San Antonio, Austin, and Washington D.C. Drs. Davis and Neumann assume that Mr. Duncan will now only be able to work as a procurement clerk in the San Antonio area with an annual salary of $38,500. Dr. Davis conjectures that it will take over two years for Mr. Duncan to obtain employment as a procurement clerk in the local metropolitan area.

Drs. Davis and Neumann's assumptions regarding Mr. Duncan's future job search are defective. If Mr. Duncan is actively and diligently seeking replacement employment, as he indicates in his disclosures in this case, he can be expected to expand his job search geographically, across different industries, and to related occupations. It is inappropriate to assume that Mr. Duncan will, and should, limit his job search to procurement clerks in the local metropolitan area.

Moreover, many of these jobs in the San Antonio area are local government jobs at the City of San Antonio. Mr. Duncan has a Master's degree from an accredited and recognized university, varied job experience, and is in the earlier stages of his working life. Mr. Duncan's Master's degree in Public Administration is applicable to any number of jobs in local, state, and federal government as well as non-profit entities and the private sector (See no. 17 in Exhibit A). It is unsound to assume that Mr. Duncan will continue to search for and work only in the same relatively low level clerk job in The City for essentially the same set of employers.

In contrast to Drs. Davis and Neumann's unsupported opinions, Mr. Duncan's discovery responses indicate that he has actually applied for jobs in cities outside of San Antonio and for job positions outside of procurement and contracting. For instance, Mr. Duncan indicated that he is applying for job positions in Washington D.C. Even if for some reason Mr. Duncan were to be limited to a procurement clerk job, the average earnings for procurement clerks is significantly higher in Washington D.C. than the earnings he could have expected from the temporary City Public Works Department job at issue in this case. It is inappropriate for Drs. Davis and Neumann not to consider Mr. Duncan's actual job search activities and employment opportunities in cities outside of the local metropolitan area where he lived.

Mr. Duncan's job search records also indicate that he is also actually applying for job positions outside of procurement clerk as conjectured by Drs. Davis and Neumann. For instance, Mr. Duncan job search records indicate that he applied for positions as a Business Analyst, Project Coordinator, Public Investment Specialist, Transportation Funding Specialist, Auditor II, and Management Analyst IV. It is likely that Mr. Duncan, who is highly educated and in the earlier stages of his work life, would be qualified to work at a number of different types of employers in a range of job positions outside of the narrow occupation of procurement clerk (See no. 18 in Exhibit A). Drs. Davis and Neumann's analyses do not take these facts into account.

Further, there was, and is, employer demand for individuals with Mr. Duncan's knowledge, skills, abilities, and experiences. Even a cursory review of the labor market for the jobs that Mr. Duncan has actually been applying for, shows that there is employer demand in the geographical areas that he has been searching. If Mr. Duncan were to expand his search into additional occupations and geographical areas the labor market data indicates additional employer demand. For instance, Mr. Duncan's job search records indicate he has submitted applications to private and public employers for jobs as a Contracts Administrator and a Purchasing Agent in the local metropolitan area. In the metropolitan area where Mr. Ducan lived, Texas Workforce Commission (TWC) and BLS labor market data tabulations indicate that in a typical month in 2012 there were approximately 179 openings for Purchasing Agents (See no. 19, 21, and 22 in Exhibit A). According to these data, there were approximately 107 searchers in a typical month in 2012. Mr. Duncan would have been at least minimally qualified to apply for any number of these positions.

The typical compensation associated with these job positions is comparable or greater to the compensation that Mr. Duncan could have been reasonably expected to earn as a temporary K-Starr employee working in the City Public Works Department. Salary data from the electronic job placement site salary.com and data from the BLS shows that the average salary in the metropolitan area for Contracts Administrator was between $50,236 and $69,530 in 2012 (See no. 23 in Exhibit A). Purchasing Agents had an average salary of $58,446 in the metropolitan area in 2012. The expected salary for these positions was higher in the other geographical areas that Mr. Duncan is targeting for employment. The expected salary for many of the job positions that Mr. Duncan has applied for is higher than the salary he could have expected to earn as a temporary employee at City.

Even a casual review of popular electronic job posting boards, such as indeed.com, simplyhired.com, monster.com, and usajobs.com, show that there are currently job openings that Mr. Duncan would be at least minimally qualified to hold (See no. 24 in Exhibit A). These job postings indicate only a portion of the employer demand that exists for Mr. Duncan's job skills since not all job openings are necessarily reflected. Some job openings are advertised through job fairs, newspaper want ads, trade industry publications, and word of mouth.

Overall, TWC and BLS data indicate that the employer demand and number of jobs available in that metropolitan area and Texas statewide will increase (See no. 18 and 20 in Exhibit A). BLS labor market data indicate that Mr. Duncan could expect to regain employment within 10 to 23 weeks (See no. 19 in Exhibit A). The unemployment rate of individuals with Mr. Duncan's level of education (3.5%) is approximately half that of the general population (6.8%) (See no. 25 in Exhibit A).

Finally, Drs. Davis and Neumann's opinions regarding the potential impact of The City letter incident on all of Mr. Duncan's future job opportunities are unsupported by case facts, sound economic reasoning, or empirical data. Dr. Davis states in his report that Mr. Duncan will "suffer a solid form of 'Stigma' based upon the actions of others." Dr. Neumann states that "Mr. Duncan faces a significant hurdle to employment if and when a potential employer sees or hears of this letter issued by his former employer."

Neither Dr. Davis nor Dr. Neumann provides case facts, academic studies, or empirical data to support their claims. Further, neither expert provides specific information concerning exactly how the letter would actually impact Mr. Duncan's future job search activities. For instance, Dr. Davis states the concept of a stigma "is now aptly applied to a wide variety of instances and tangible objects, as well as human beings whose lives, careers, families, ventures and income earning potential or other assets have been damaged by an outside 'incident'." However Dr. Davis provides no studies, data, case facts or anything to demonstrate how Mr. Duncan has in fact been damaged in this case by a stigma of any type.

Similarly, Dr. Neumann states in his report that The City letter presents the "same problem is found by released public offenders trying to return to the labor market. An aura of suspicion and distrust tends to follow the job applicant with this history." However, Dr. Neumann provides no studies, data, case facts or anything to demonstrate how The City letter in this case is actually similar to having one's identity in a publically accessible offender's database. Dr. Neumann does not even discuss how The City letter would be discovered, or if the letter has in fact been discovered, by Mr. Duncan's potential employers.

It is my understanding that The City letter was not issued as part of a public record such as an arrest record, jail record, public offender registry, or police report. It is unreasonable to assume that The City letter would be discovered through a background check. It is also my understanding that The City letter is not included in Mr. Duncan's confidential personnel file with the City. Even if The City letter was included in his confidential personnel file, it is unreasonable to assume that Mr. Duncan's private and confidential information would even be discovered by potential employers.

Neither Dr. Davis nor Dr. Neumann indicates that Mr. Duncan's confidential and personal information has in fact been released or even requested by a potential employer since The City letter incident. Further, I have also been informed that City's employment policies do not provide for the release of personnel files in the manner suggested by Drs. Davis and Neumann. Drs. Davis and Neumann's assumption is even less plausible for employers outside of local government and in the private sector.

Index

A
Ad rate, 67
American Community Survey (ACS), 68, 69
American Time Use Survey (ATUS), 59, 69
Attrition rate, 61, 62

B
Back pay, 4, 5, 47, 58, 107, 108
BLS Occupational Outlook Handbook (OOH), 38, 39, 105, 110
Blue collar jobs, 66
Bureau of Labor Statistics (BLS), 12, 13, 21–24, 34–36, 45–48, 58, 64, 69–73, 98, 99, 103, 105, 124, 125, 132, 146, 148
But-for, 2, 3, 5, 7–11, 22, 61, 91, 142, 145

C
Census of Fatal Occupational Injuries, 70
Compensation, monetary, 8
Compensation, non-wage. *See* Fringe benefits
Consumer Expenditure Survey (CEX), 70
Consumer Price Index (CPI), 70, 71
Current Employment Statistics (CES), 71

D
Dictionary of Occupational Titles, 73
Diligent job search, 31, 34, 38, 48, 95, 96, 99, 102, 104, 119, 125, 132, 138

E
Economic damage, 1–5, 21, 22, 24, 28, 51, 52, 54, 71, 76–79,

© The Editor(s) (if applicable) and The Author(s), under exclusive license to Springer Nature Switzerland AG 2022
D. Steward, *Economic Losses and Mitigation after an Employment Termination*,
https://doi.org/10.1007/978-3-030-88364-5

81–83, 86, 121, 122, 127, 128, 135, 141, 142
Employment termination, 1–4, 7–11, 14, 17, 21, 23, 27–32, 36–38, 47, 51, 53, 58, 73, 89–93, 101, 127, 138
Equal Employment Opportunity Census (EEO Census), 72, 73

F
Fringe benefits
  401(k), 20
  health insurance, 2, 8, 12, 13, 49, 144
  IRA, SIMPLE, 20
  life insurance, 8, 12, 13
  retirement contributions. *See* Retirement benefits
  stock. *See* Stock based compensation
Front pay, 2, 4, 5, 28, 48, 51, 54, 57, 90, 92, 141, 142
Future income, 53

H
Historical earnings, 8, 18

I
Illiquidity discount, 85, 86
Interest rate, 4, 15, 53, 54, 80
Interest rate discount factor, 4, 5, 51–55, 79
Intrinsic value analysis, 78, 81

J
Job churn, 62, 63
Job evaluations, 67, 68
Job openings, 33, 44, 45, 47, 64–66, 72, 98, 103, 117, 119, 124, 131, 132, 139, 148

Job Openings and Labor Turnover Survey (JOLTS), 64–67, 72
Job tenure, 3, 8, 21–24, 55, 60, 61, 63, 64, 71, 128, 131, 136, 146

L
Labor market, 9, 12, 21, 29, 30, 32, 34, 35, 37–39, 43–47, 57, 59, 65, 67, 72, 95–97, 99, 102, 110, 112, 115–117, 119, 121, 124, 125, 127, 128, 131, 132, 135, 136, 141, 142, 146–149
Local Area Unemployment Statistics, 72
Lump sum, 18, 53

M
Mitigation analysis, 28, 59–62, 131
Monetary allowances, 12

N
National Longitudinal Survey of Youth (NLSY), 62, 72, 73

O
Occupational Information Network, 73
Opportunity occupations, 66

P
Panel Study of Income Dynamics (PSID), 73
Pension plans. *See* Retirement plans, defined benefit
Post-termination employment, 31, 58, 64, 138
Present value, 2–5, 51–54, 58, 90
Projected earnings, 3, 5, 7, 25, 91

R

Re-employment, 2, 27, 50, 131
Replacement employment, comparable, 1, 28, 29, 39, 47, 57, 95, 96, 119, 125, 131, 132, 138
Replacement value, 12
Retention rate, 62
Retirement, 1–3, 8, 17–21, 25, 49, 50, 52, 60, 61, 90, 91, 144
Retirement benefits, 12, 13, 17, 47, 135, 136
Retirement plans, defined benefit, 17–19, 22, 92, 116
Retirement plans, defined contribution, 17, 19, 20, 92, 116

S

Salary fringe benefit multiplier, 12
Social security contributions, 12
Stock based compensation, 13, 17, 75–77, 131
Stock options (ESO), 2, 8, 13–17, 30, 75–86, 92, 116
Stock option valuation, 76
 Black Scholes model (B-S), 79, 81
 Black Scholes, modified Shapiro and O'Connor model, 79, 86
 Lattice tree model, Hull and White, 79, 81, 82
Stock price, grant, 14, 15, 17, 81, 84
Stock price, spot, 79
Stock price, strike, 78
Stock purchase plans, 13, 16, 17, 75
Stock redemption behavior, 84

T

Tenure projections, 21
The Help Wanted Online Data Series (HWOL), 45, 65
Time value of money, 3, 52, 80
Turnover, employee, 15, 46, 63

U

Underemployment, 49, 99
Unemployment duration, 47–49, 60
Unemployment insurance, 12, 34
Universe of Employers, 44
US Census, 68–71
U.S. Current Population Survey (CPS), 22, 58, 59, 61, 64, 71, 98, 132

W

White collar jobs, 66
Worker's compensation insurance, 12
Work life, 21, 22, 52, 60, 147
Wrongful employment termination, 2

CPSIA information can be obtained
at www.ICGtesting.com
Printed in the USA
LVHW081928230822
726670LV00001B/2

9 783030 883638